DARWIN COMES
TO AFRICA

DARWIN COMES TO AFRICA

SOCIAL DARWINISM AND BRITISH
IMPERIALISM IN NORTHERN NIGERIA

OLUFEMI OLUNIYI

SEATTLE   DISCOVERY INSTITUTE PRESS   2023

Description

Charles Darwin fathered not just a scientific theory, but a toxic social ideology that fueled racist colonial policies in Africa. In this sobering book, African scholar Olufemi Oluniyi traces the insidious impact of Darwinian ideas on British imperial policies in Northern Nigeria. Drawing on official documents, public statements, and well-attested historical events, Oluniyi documents how concepts such as evolutionary racism and survival of the fittest were systematically used to demean black Africans, consigning some people to a status of permanent inferiority. Rejecting Social Darwinism, Oluniyi makes a compelling argument for the equality of all human beings, and for recognizing Africa's many seminal contributions to the history of human civilization.

Copyright Notice

Library Cataloging Data

Darwin Comes to Africa: Social Darwinism and British Imperialism in Northern Nigeria by Olufemi Oluniyi

Cover design by Brian Gage. Interior by Mike Perry.

192 pages, 6 x 9 x 0.4 in & 0.6 lb, 229 x 152 x 10.4 mm & 266 g

Library of Congress Control Number: 9781637120231

ISBN: 978-1-63712-023-1 (paperback), 978-1-63712-025-5 (Kindle), 978-1-63712-024-8 (EPUB)

BISAC:

SOC056000 SOCIAL SCIENCE/Black Studies (Global)

SOC070000 SOCIAL SCIENCE/Race & Ethnic Relations

POL045000 POLITICAL SCIENCE/Colonialism & Post-Colonialism

POL047000 POLITICAL SCIENCE/Imperialism

HIS014000 HISTORY/Africa/West

SCI034000 SCIENCE/History

Publisher Information

Discovery Institute Press, 208 Columbia Street, Seattle, WA 98104
Internet: discoveryinstitutepress.com

Published in the United States of America on acid-free paper.

First edition, February 2023.

ADVANCE PRAISE

This book exposes the horrifying extent to which Social Darwinist principles and policies mutilated Northern Nigeria. The author vividly uncovers how British colonizers used Social Darwinism to label Africans as biologically inferior beings lower on the evolutionary ladder, creating a fertile ground for manipulation, oppression, and exploitation. As the book clearly demonstrates, the objectives of Social Darwinism were denigration, subjugation, exploitation, and dehumanization. The author powerfully challenges evolutionary arguments for racism. He also refutes Western myths about the history of Africa as the "dark continent," recounting Africa's many contributions to ancient manufacturing, medicine, architecture, mathematics, and more. Overall, the book presents an inspiring vision of the transcendent value of all people as equal members of the same human race.

—Richard Ochieng', PhD, Lecturer and Deputy Director, Academic and Student Affairs, University of Eldoret, Kenya; Chair, BioCosmos Kenya Trust Foundation

In this interesting and informative book, Oluniyi examines the ideological underpinnings of British imperialism in Nigeria, providing a powerful reminder that Social Darwinism and the scientific racism flowing from it had profoundly damaging influences on real people, especially those—such as black Africans—denigrated by scientific elites as "inferior" on the evolutionary ladder.

—Richard Weikart, Professor Emeritus of History at California State University, Stanislaus; Senior Fellow of Discovery Institute's Center for Science and Culture; and author of *Darwinian Racism: How Darwinism Influenced Hitler, Nazism, and White Nationalism*

Debates over the meaning of Darwin's work are often treated as merely academic—they have little practical influence on people's lives. *Darwin Comes to Africa* puts the lie to this by documenting in vivid detail the role played by Social Darwinism in providing an intellectual foundation for British colonial exploitation of Northern Nigeria, and Africa more generally. Steeped in a white supremacist mindset founded on Darwinian principles, British colonial masters ironically created the very African inferiority they believed in by actively undermining Nigerian advancements in politics, economics, education, and culture. Oluniyi brilliantly paints a picture of why "scientific" theories like Darwinism matter in the real world.

—Robert F. Shedinger, PhD, Wilford A. Johnson Chair in Biblical Studies and Professor of Religion, Luther College; author of *The Mystery of Evolutionary Mechanisms: Darwinian Biology's Grand Narrative of Triumph and the Subversion of Religion*

There are many aspects to the disturbing story of Social Darwinism. Originating with Darwin's infatuation with the craniometry of Paul Broca and Joseph Barnard Davis, his brand of reductionist evolutionary theory could easily be wedded to preexisting self-serving racial and ethnic prejudices to create a dark and evil "science" that has destroyed millions of lives. Here the late Olufemi Oluniyi tells of the impact upon his native Nigeria primarily through the misguided policies of British colonial administrator Frederick Lugard who, in Oluniyi's words, was "a key figure in the degradation of Nigeria and, moreover, of Africa at large." Much of this was done in the name of "science" and Darwinian evolution. The book, however, is more than the story of one misguided colonialist; it gives important context and detail to the unfortunate African experience with Darwinism in general. Here the ghost of Alfred Russel Wallace, the co-discoverer of natural selection who rejected Darwinian evolution, speaks afresh through Oluniyi, harkening to his disgust in 1906 at British colonialism in South Africa. Its policy, he declared, resulted "in the degradation and lingering extermination of so fine a people," making it "one of the most pathetic of its tragedies." *Darwin Comes to Africa* is a disconcerting but valuable historical, scientific, sociological, and political commentary on the tragic intersection of Social Darwinism and indigenous peoples.

—Michael A. Flannery, author of *Nature's Prophet: Alfred Russel Wallace and His Evolution from Natural Selection to Natural Theology* (2018) and *Intelligent Evolution: How Alfred Russel Wallace's* World of Life *Challenged Darwinism* (2020)

Ideas rule the world, and corrosive ideologies damage human relations and destroy societies. In this book, Olufemi Oluniyi lucidly exposes how the pseudo-science of Social Darwinism fueled manipulative and exploitative British imperialist policies in Northern Nigeria to damage human relations and destroy societies. The book clearly demonstrates how British colonizers, led by Lord and Lady Lugard, were fully imbued with the ideology of Social Darwinism of the time, which supported the development of scientific racism. This ideology enabled the imperialists and colonizers in Africa to erroneously redefine "fitness" in evolutionary theory as "intelligence," and "intelligence" as "white" and its close associate "light or fair-skinned." Thus, British colonizers quickly singled out and labeled the fair-skinned Muslim Fulani people of Northern Nigeria as "superior" on the evolutionary ladder, and therefore, as the supposed rulers over their black or dark-skinned counterparts. The author exposes the pseudo-scientific basis of evolutionary arguments for racism and vividly shows how British Social Darwinist policies were a root cause of the damaged relations among the peoples of Nigeria. This root cause continues to exert its influence in Nigeria's effort to build a sustainable democracy in the twenty-first century. In all, Oluniyi's book is interesting, inspiring, and highly informative, and its narrative is captivating.

—Mary-Noelle Ethel Ezeh IHM, Professor of Ethics and Christian History, Chukwuemeka Odumegwu Ojukwu University, Nigeria

Shocking and eye-opening. This book documents the tragic consequences of exporting Darwin's ideas to Africa, consequences Nigeria is still living with today.

—John G. West, PhD, Vice President, Discovery Institute, and author of *Darwin Day in America*

CONTENTS

FOREWORD

John G. West

LIKE MOST WHITE AMERICANS, I HAVE NOT SPENT MUCH OF MY LIFE thinking about or studying Africa and its rich history. I say this with regret.

My insularity was challenged when I met the author of this book.

Rev. Dr. Olufemi Oluniyi came to Seattle in the summer of 2017 to participate in Discovery Institute's C. S. Lewis Fellows Program on Science and Society, which I direct. The trip ended up being Olufemi's first and only visit to America. Although offered a visiting research professorship at the Catholic University of America years earlier, Olufemi had not been able to accept it at the time.

Olufemi opened my eyes and heart to the importance of Nigeria to Africa, the dynamic role of Christians there, and the importance of Africa to the world. His joy for life, his love for his home country, and his love for his fellow man were contagious.

Olufemi led an influential life. He served as a Christian minister, a college professor and administrator, a journalist, and an activist for peace and non-violence.

He came to participate in our summer seminar program because he was especially interested in the impact of Social Darwinism and scientism on society. He had already touched on the topic in his book *Reconciliation in Northern Nigeria: The Space for Public Apology*, but now he hoped to dig deeper.

Only later did I learn that Olufemi had been filled with trepidation about his trip to America. He knew that Americans tend to focus on themselves, and he wasn't sure his contributions would be valued. He also worried that Discovery Institute might have a blind spot—focusing too narrowly on the scientific debates over Darwinian theory to the exclusion of its social impact.

I'm happy to say that after coming to Seattle he realized he had found kindred spirits. He later wrote:

> As I understand it, Discovery Institute is a spearhead for the reclamation of (1) who we are as human beings, and (2) what we are as human society, from the increasingly compulsive characteristic of desperate Darwinism. Undoubtedly [it is] an American organization, hence it cannot evade matters American... However, in terms of its primal and primary commitment, it is a global alignment of like minds. It epitomizes a firm rejection of that concentrated falsehood—Darwinism—about (1) who we are as human beings. It equally abhors its vacuous and baseless derivative—Social Darwinism—which parades itself in the academe on (2) what we are as human society. If you prefer a different figure of speech, Discovery Institute is comparable to a spring. It exudes fresh information, brimming with facts and figures over claims which Darwinism has foreclosed. It calls the bluff in broad daylight for Darwinism in its vaunted materialist mode to pick up the gauntlet.

I learned much from Olufemi that summer, and he awoke in me an abiding interest in both the history and future of Africa. As for Olufemi, he found renewed inspiration to further his investigations of Social Darwinism. By the end of the seminar, he had decided to write a book focusing on the impact of Social Darwinism in Nigeria and refuting its falsehoods. "I announced at the closing session of the seminar my resolve to write a book on Social Darwinism," he later recalled. "That announcement was a way of self-bolstering my resolve to write and not to renege on the resolve."

In the years that followed, Olufemi and I exchanged hundreds of emails as he shared his progress in his research. As he worked on his book, he found himself reflecting on connections between his own life and the life of Charles Darwin:

> No sooner had I begun my research in earnest than I realized that Charles Darwin and I crisscrossed in our life journeys, with the University of Edinburgh, Scotland, the oldest civic university in the British Empire, as the nexus. On the comparison column, both of us had theological-pastoral training, he at Cambridge University, England, and I at SIM/ECWA Theological Seminary, Igbaja, Nigeria, respectively. Again, in the comparison column, both of us had Edinburgh University education; he in medicine and I in political theology, though at different levels; he at the undergraduate level; I at master's level. In contrast, sadly, Darwin failed his course, whereas I passed mine.
>
> Nevertheless, both of us seem to have come away with the spirit of adventure that Edinburgh University seems to stamp on students that come within its walls. Indeed, my one-year stint in New College is an abiding inspiration—excellent professors and lecturers sharing knowledge and making themselves available, without a tinge of snobbery, staff that readily cooperate all year round, lunch time fellowships with academicians who stop by, proximity to the National Library of Scotland, etc.…

But "whereas Darwin's adventure took him down the slippery slope of that pseudo-science of natural selection," explained Olufemi, "I emerged as an entrenched critic of the rickety notion of Social Darwinism."

Olufemi finished a full draft of his manuscript in June 2021. Ever enthusiastic, he wrote me at the time: "I ask myself, why can't this book make it to the *New York Times* book of the year?" We continued to correspond about his book and other matters into July. Then, strangely, he fell silent. I learned later he had caught COVID-19. On August 2, he died from its complications.

When my father died in 2019, I found a verse in the Bible that gave me comfort, and I think it applies equally well to Olufemi: "Blessed are the dead who die in the Lord… they will rest from their labors, for their deeds follow them" (Rev. 14:13).

Olufemi's friendship was a great blessing in my life, and I wish you could have known him. Through this book, you can get a glimpse.

I would like to thank Amanda Witt for her careful editing work, which allowed this book to be finalized for publication even in the absence of its author; historian Richard Weikart for his peer review of the manuscript; Mike Perry for the book's typesetting and layout; and Peter Biles for preparing the index. Finally, I would like to thank Olufemi Oluniyi's wife and children for supporting posthumous publication of his important book.

Dr. Oluniyi's own acknowledgments appear later in this book.

John G. West
Vice President
Discovery Institute

PREFACE

SOCIAL DARWINISM IS A RICKETY NOTION, RICH IN ASSUMPTIONS but destitute of facts. It reminds me of a Mandinka proverb widely recognized in Africa which says, "An empty bag cannot stand." It is, however, resourceful. Social Darwinism rests like a tiger moth on Darwinism, its mother theory; when challenged with facts, it flits to a slightly different position and poses anew, where its camouflaging coloration allows it to survive a bit longer.

However, Social Darwinism is not merely as tricky and insubstantial as a tiger moth. It also is as dangerous as a tiger. As shall be shown in these pages, a large portion of Northern Nigeria's suffering can be laid directly at the feet of this tiger and its parent. This book is an invitation to readers, and to African scholars particularly, to look around them and determine to what extent Social Darwinism has mauled their respective societies and nations.

What precisely is this dangerous creature? Though it goes by many camouflaging names, Social Darwinism is the pseudo-scientific ideology which posits that the biological principles of Darwin's scientific theory of random mutation and natural selection bear analogy to human society.

One startling iteration of Social Darwinism occurred under the guise of tactical warfare in the 1920s, when Russian scientist Ilya Ivanovich Ivanov sought to produce a race of super-soldiers for Stalin's army by impregnating French Guinea women with the sperm of a dead chimpanzee—black African women, mind you, who were presumed to be less highly evolved and thus closer to chimpanzees than were white European women. The Russian scientist was not a lone gunman, so to speak.

Colonial authorities approved the plan, and the Russian found support amongst both French and American scientists, the latter of which "expressed opposition to impregnating chimps with human sperm because of animal-welfare considerations but was not opposed to impregnating African women with sperm from a chimpanzee." Moreover, "there were no plans to tell the women what they would be carrying."[1]

Horrifying though this experiment is in terms of religion and morality, it makes ethical sense under Social Darwinism. If humans are naught but evolutionarily advanced animals, and if we breed and crossbreed animals to suit our purposes, why should we not breed humans in the same manner?

Darwin's theory of evolution further posited the natural world as a place where the fittest survive and the less-fit decline and die; if this is indeed the case, thought Darwin's contemporaries (and indeed many of our own), then who are we to battle nature herself? Why should we not let the less-fit die? Indeed, why should we not hasten their demise if it will profit us—the survivors, the fittest—economically, geographically, or politically? Why should the Briton not manipulate, oppress, and exploit the Nigerian? After all, the fact that he can do so surely proves that he is *right* to do so—he is fulfilling his very destiny, as decreed by Nature herself.

True, such predatory impulses are as old as man himself. This book, however, explores the nineteenth-century attempt to repackage those age-old myths, prejudices, racism, and general selfishness in a pseudo-scientific wrapper.

That pseudo-scientific wrapper has allowed myriad evils to flourish up to the present day. Without doubt, Darwin's scientific theory of evolution and its social ramifications, though unproven and indeed increasingly discredited, hold pernicious sway in classrooms and boardrooms, in the halls of politics, medicine, and trade.

Though the objective of Social Darwinism was and still is the denigration, subjugation, exploitation, and dehumanization of targeted peoples, these evils generally are cloaked in the benevolent language of guiding an inferior race or protecting a superior one by weeding out supposedly inferior stock. At various times and in various places people so targeted have been the mentally or physically disabled, the elderly, the ill, the homosexual, the unborn;[2] those whose ethnicity, nationality, or appearance has posed a real or perceived barrier to the fulfilment of another group's desires;[3] and those whose poverty or criminality has been blamed, Darwinist-fashion, upon inferior genetics. The problems of Social Darwinism are various and are pervasive worldwide,[4] and all people wronged by Darwin and his followers deserve to have their stories told and the false narratives wielded against them deconstructed. My focus in these pages, however, will be on my people and my country.

Here is how the idea of a nineteenth-century scientist traveled four thousand miles to grievously wound Northern Nigeria: Charles Darwin emerged at a time when Europe and Great Britain were hungry for an excuse to exploit Africa. Darwin's theories provided a morally palatable (though as we shall see, entirely wrong and illogical) excuse. Further, in addition to justifying self-serving colonization, Darwin's theories shaped the way British administrators managed Northern Nigeria and the various people groups therein.

The false narrative of Social Darwinism as promoted by British colonizers caused great and unjust harm to Nigeria, and to this day many aspects of the pernicious narrative are widely and harmfully believed to be true. However, the critical link between the increasingly insatiable appetite for Africa's resources, on the one hand, and Charles Darwin's growing visibility, on the other hand, has been ignored, as if willfully, in the conventional Social Darwinist historiography. I will present ample evidence for my claims in Part One of this book, drawing on official documents, public statements, well-attested historical events, and so forth.

This book does not deny that there are differences in material culture, literacy, and technological attainments between Europe and Black Africa; rather, it firmly rejects the sleight of hand that these external differences indicate a difference in the basic building blocks of the European and of the African (understood to mean black-skinned Africans), and that this supposed inherent difference causes cultural differences and warrants "Europeans are superior to Africans" propaganda. These matters I shall discuss in Part Two of this book.

My purpose is not merely to point the finger of blame, nor is it merely to restore a view of the black African as equal in all ways to the white European. It is also to show that Social Darwinism rests on a faulty foundation, so that perhaps the day may come when the House of Darwin and all his unruly, self-serving children harm no longer.

PART ONE:
DARWIN COMES TO AFRICA

Figure 1.1. Charles Darwin caricatured as an "orang-outang" by the satirical magazine *The Hornet* in 1871.

1. DARWINIAN IMPERIALISM

A FRICA IS A CONTINENT RICH IN NATURAL RESOURCES. FOR MANY long centuries Africa was plagued by slave traders, and when finally interest in slave-trading waned (for practical economic as much as moral reasons), interest in Africa's wealth did not. By the mid-nineteenth century Europe was hungry to partake of Africa's abundant mineral and agricultural resources. What began ostensibly as the search for Timbuktu and the course of the River Niger, as a geographical project in the last quarter of the eighteenth century, increasingly concentrated on the potential commercial returns of those explorations. Documentation of markets, goods, resources, and services increased the number of sponsors of prospective explorations. The more raw materials Europeans came across, the greater the appetite for compulsive acquisition of those African resources. Because America had at this time withdrawn from the slave trade and become focused on westward expansion, Europe had no external competitor. Africa was there for the taking.

Into this climate came Charles Darwin, whose framework of ideas provided an ostensibly moral and scientific justification for the plundering of Africa.

From Science to Society

ALLOW ME now to present an overview of the unfolding of that process by which Darwinism in the historical realm of origins science became Social Darwinism in the realm of human interactions, resulting in a host of societal ills, not least of which has been the subjugation and degradation of my country.

In 1859 Darwin's first book, *On the Origin of Species,* was published. This book framed life as a struggle in which the fittest organisms survive and reproduce, while the weakest die. This he called "natural selection." (Darwin did not create the term "survival of the fittest"—Herbert Spencer first used the term in 1852—but there is no doubt that Darwin both admired and popularized the term and the concept.[1]) Significantly, the *Origin* presented humans as highly developed animals. In Chapter 3, for example, titled "The Struggle for Existence," Darwin mentions "slow-breeding man."

Breeding a Better Human

READERS AROUND the world were quick to see the implications. By 1865 Darwin's cousin Frances Galton had written articles for *MacMillan's* magazine and by 1869 published the book *Hereditary Genius,* laying the groundwork for the eugenics movement, which focused on breeding healthier human specimens and weeding out weaker specimens (Galton himself coined the term "eugenics" in 1883, derived from the Greek for "well born.")

According to historian Richard Weikart, biologist Ernst Haeckel (1834–1919) considered "the animal ancestry of humanity the most important aspect of evolutionary theory"[2] and did not hesitate to apply Darwin's idea of struggle for existence to human society. Notes Weikart, Haeckel believed "this struggle is a progressive force in human history, since it contributes to the development of new and higher forms."[3]

The aforementioned Herbert Spencer, according to Rutledge M. Dennis, "reasoned that Darwinist principles were intended to buttress the case that biological evolution could be equally applicable to human societies." Further, Dennis explains, Spencer reasoned

> that human societies, like biological species, operate according to the principles of natural selection, are governed by competition and fitness, and evolve from an undifferentiated (homogenous) and primitive state to one of differentiation (heterogeneity) and progress. Those too weak or ill-equipped to compete, or those who are unwilling or unable to do

so, he reasoned, ought not to be given an artificial boost to keep them on Nature's battlefield.[4]

Of course not all scientists were willing to make the leap from biology to human society, but many did.[5] Eventually this application of Darwinian theory to human society led to compulsory sterilization laws designed to prevent the reproduction of the physically "defective" and mentally "feeble," and also of the morally deficient or criminal. British eugenicists passed the British Lunacy Act of 1904, the Royal Commission on the Care and Control of the Feeble-Minded in 1908, and the Mental Deficiency Bill in 1912–13, all of which sought to strengthen Britain's mental health via sterilization and/or containment of the mentally ill or deficient.[6] Other countries[7] actually enacted compulsory sterilization laws to advance eugenics, including Sweden,[8] the United States,[9] and of course Germany, which with its Nazi party went so far as to euthanize the "unfit" in aid of producing a healthier German people.[10]

Thus the application of Darwinism to society made it acceptable to rank human life according to a value system of power and strength. Moreover, it was the species that mattered, while "individual human lives were not really so important."[11] Put baldly, "Darwin's particular theory of evolution by natural selection contributed to a devaluing of human life."[12]

Exterminating "Lower" Races

DARWIN ALSO elevated race as a factor in the struggle for survival. Twelve years after the publication of *On the Origin of Species*, in 1871, Darwin published *The Descent of Man and Selection in Relation to Sex*, a highly impactful book as far as Europe's attitudes to Africa. Professor Frank Besag observes that in Darwin's first book, he used "race" and "species" interchangeably. In other words, at that time "for Darwin, there was a human race but not a black race."[13] Or at least Darwin chose, in his earlier book, not to explicitly bring up such a controversial idea. The implications, however, were clear; thus Dennis notes that "the philosophical and political underpinnings of ideas associated with racial superiority and inferiority were first given scientific legitimacy and credence with the publication of Charles Darwin's (1859) revolutionary book, *The Origin of Species.*"[14]

In his second book, however, Darwin not only made references to races among humans, but he further distinguished between "the lowest savages" and "the lowest barbarians"[15] on the one hand, and the "highly civilised nations,"[16] including "the Western nations of Europe, who... stand at the summit of civilisation"[17] on the other.

Two points of clarification are here required. First, while at times Darwin used the terms "savages" and "barbarians" to refer to the modern human's ancient forebears, at other times he used those derogatory terms to speak of his contemporaries in distant lands, as when he writes, "At the present day civilised nations are everywhere supplanting barbarous nations, excepting where the climate opposes a deadly barrier; and they succeed mainly, though not exclusively, through their arts, which are the products of the intellect. It is, therefore, highly probable that with mankind the intellectual faculties have been gradually perfected through natural selection."[18]

Second, as has been most indisputably and thoroughly documented elsewhere,[19] Darwin's letters and other writings clearly demonstrate that by "barbarous," "inferior," or "lower" peoples he usually meant dark-skinned people. The terms "highly civilised" or "superior" he applied to Caucasians. For example, in *The Descent of Man* Darwin states that the black man is closer than the white man to apes,[20] and speaks of "the Negro" who "differs more... from the other races of man than do the mammals of the same continents from those of the other provinces."[21] There can be no doubt that Darwin thought dark-skinned peoples were less highly evolved than light-skinned peoples.

Racism (the dividing of humans on the supposed basis of race) did of course exist before Darwin. By 1779 German physiologist Johann Friedrich Blumenbach had divided humankind into five races based on cranial features, while by 1759 Swedish botanist Carl Linnaeus had classified human beings into four categories based on the four known continents

(European white, American reddish, Asian tawny, African black).[22] The Frenchman Joseph Arthur de Gobineau classified humans into three racial groups by 1855 (black, white, and yellow).[23]

Nevertheless, what the classifications lacked was a more credible scientific basis, which Darwin ostensibly provided. (Later we shall speak more of these foolish and harmful divisions and show that they have no basis in reality, but that rather there is only one human race, of which we are all a part.)

In the aftermath of Darwin's books, as Gregory Claeys notes, Social Darwinism redefined fitness as intelligence, and intelligence as white—and let it be noted that "Darwin accepted the application... with others following suit, crafting a language of exclusion... [and] racial conflict." In short, within a few years of Darwin's books, "much of the language of ethnicity which would come to haunt the next century was now in place."[24]

Thus we see, summarizes Weikart, the biologist Wilhelm Roux (1850–1924) describing the Darwinian "struggle within organisms as analogous to the struggle within society."[25] Similarly, writes Weikart, paleontologist Friedrich Rolle (1827–1887) argued that "population pressure naturally precipitates wars and violent conflicts between peoples and races" and that "the physically and mentally superior races suppress and exterminate the lower races, bringing progress and benefit to the whole of mankind."[26]

Likewise the biologist Heinrich Ziegler (1891–1918) advocated that "according to Darwin's theory, war has constantly been of the greatest importance for the general progress of the human race" and that "the physically weaker, the less intelligent, the morally inferior or morally degenerate peoples must clear out and make room for the stronger and better developed"[27] in the interest of the general progress of the human race.

According to Weikart, Darwin's disciple Haeckel differentiated "between ten races of humanity, with the Caucasian race the most highly developed," following which he fervently "condoned the extermination of" so-called primitive races.[28] Similarly, zoologist Oscar Schmidt

(1823–1886), zoologist Richard Hertwig (1850–1937), biologist Richard Semon (1859–1918), and biologist Ernst Krause (1839–1903) all advocated "the extermination of human races as a natural and inevitable part of the process of natural selection."[29]

You see what we have here. These men and likewise many others argued that the logical extrapolation of Darwin's theory was the extermination of their fellow humans in the name of evolutionary progress!

Darwin and Social Darwinism

LET ME here pause to acknowledge that Darwin was not alone to blame for the ills of what later came to be called Social Darwinism—the belief that biological laws apply to man as well as to animals and organisms, and that therefore population growth results in a competition-to-the-death for resources and space; that inherited traits confer advantages or disadvantages on their possessors in this struggle; and that the cumulative work of selection and inheritance over time results in the emergence of new species and the elimination of others. Others before and alongside Darwin, including for example Thomas Malthus, contributed to these notions. As Claeys notes, "what was specific about much of Social Darwinism resulted from several shifts in thought in mid-Victorian Britain to which Darwin himself also responded and which therefore also vitally influenced his own development."[30]

However, as Claeys also writes, "Darwin was extraordinarily widely read and extraordinarily influential"[31] and, by the 1860s, was himself a thoroughgoing Social Darwinist who "accepted the application of natural selection to humanity," even if that application was not entirely of his own making.[32]

To give one example, in the *Descent* Darwin expressed disapproval of primogeniture, the British system of inheritance that favored the eldest male. Because of it, he wrote, "most eldest sons, though they may be weak in body or mind, marry."[33] In other words, the inheritance system goes against natural selection by encouraging the weak to breed.

Thus, when drawing the line between Darwin and Social Darwinism, Claeys is right to conclude the "assertion of causation contains some truth."[34] Darwin pulled together many threads, tied them neatly into a more credible scientific theory of his own design, and presented them to the world in a comprehensive and quasi-scientific package. Thus while Social Darwinism cannot be blamed solely on Charles Darwin, it is wholly reasonable that his name represent the package of resulting ills.

While Western culture at large embraced Darwin's scientific theory and its application to human society, some of Darwin's contemporaries argued against Darwin's view of human origins, evolutionary development, and race as expressed in his books. A great number of Christians recognized that whether or not Darwinism as a historical science was true (and, as we shall see, it was not), the Social Darwinist principles growing from it were inimical to true Christianity. Nevertheless, despite these objections, Darwin's scientific ideas were rapidly assimilated into the social and political realm and used to justify various *might makes right* doctrines.

Darwinism and Militarism

IT IS indisputable that later in the nineteenth century, "advocates of imperialism, racism, and eugenics began relying on Darwinist arguments."[35] Claeys points out that "the language of race in the *Descent* is overlaid almost exactly on an earlier, familiar language of savagery and civility, which was itself central to the existing justification of imperial expansion."[36]

Darwin himself, as evidenced by remarks in the *Descent*, saw British imperialism as a progressive force of natural selection. In Chapter 7 of that book, in a section titled "The Extinction of Races," he describes the decline in various "wild" populations caused by contact with Europeans. He writes:

> Extinction follows chiefly from the competition of tribe with tribe, and race with race.... The contest is soon settled by war, slaughter, cannibalism, slavery, and absorption. Even when a weaker tribe is not thus

abruptly swept away, if once it begins to decrease, it generally goes on decreasing until it is extinct.

When civilised nations come into contact with barbarians the struggle is short.... The grade of civilisation seems a most important element in the success of nations which come in competition.[37]

Indeed, Darwin wrote approvingly that "at some future period, not very distant as measured by centuries, the civilised races of man will almost certainly exterminate and replace throughout the world the savage races."[38]

And who are the savage races? Two sentences later Darwin notes that the negro or Australian (by which he meant the aborigine) is the closest human form to the gorilla.

Thus Darwin's *Descent of Man*, arriving as it did at a crucial moment in the European appetite for Africa, assumed great significance because it allowed the discourse to shift from resources to race, and allowed a means of rationalizing the intrusion of "superior" races into the lives of the "inferior" ones. As Dennis notes, "Social Darwinism was accepted in England and the United States because it supported policies and practices that both countries justified as congruent with their national interests."[39]

Let us now see what that meant for Africa.

Figure 2.1. Representatives of the European powers at the Berlin Conference in 1884.

2. The "Inferior African" Narrative

By the middle of the nineteenth century, European nations were in need of natural resources for their growing industries, and also in need of potential markets for the goods their industries produced. Africa seemed to offer precisely what the European nations desired. They perceived Africa as being un-owned, for African states were not regarded as legitimate entities, but were considered primitive societies inhabited by barbaric dark-skinned peoples who stood lower on the evolutionary ladder than did their white European counterparts. (In Part Two we shall dismantle the "evolutionary ladder" and "primitive societies" myths.)

In order to avoid shedding one another's blood in their competition over the continent, in 1884 the heads of state from thirteen European countries and the United States came together at Berlin to discuss who should control Africa's resources.[1] No African representatives were present. This conference, known variously as the Berlin Conference, the Congo Conference, or the West African Conference, sought to regulate European colonization and trade in Africa. The conference lasted for three months, until February 1885, and the tug-of-war continued afterwards as well.

This was the climax of the so-called "Scramble for Africa," during which seven European powers (Belgium, France, Germany, Great Britain, Italy, Portugal, and Spain) invaded, annexed, conquered, colonized, and came to control most of Africa. Before the Berlin Conference, some

80 percent of Africa remained under local control. By 1914 only 10 percent remained free from European control. Only Ethiopia (then called Abyssinia) and Liberia remained independent, and even so, Liberia was tied closely to the United States, and Ethiopia would fall to Italy in 1936.

In the treaty-making arrangement at the Berlin Conference, European nations invoked the "sphere of influence" principle. Several factors contributed to the British claim of a "sphere of influence" in the Lower Niger, which led the Berlin Conference to concede the Lower Niger to the British. First, Britain had signed trade treaties with the coastal peoples of the Bight of Biafra, which Britain converted to a political treaty in 1885. Second, the presence of the Church Missionary Society Christian missionaries in the Badagry-Abeokuta axis on the one hand and the Scottish missionaries in the Calabar-Akwa Ibom axis on the other were presented as evidence of a British sphere of influence. Also, an English trading company which at the time was called the African National Company (later to be called the Royal Niger Company) maintained a near-monopoly in the Lower Niger.

It is, however, significant to note that the Berlin Conference made no reference to the Upper Niger. No European power fulfilled the requirements for a "sphere of influence" over Northern Nigeria, and therefore, Northern Nigeria was open to "the survival of the fittest" among European nations. The three most powerful Western European powers of the day, Britain, France, and Germany, thereafter swung into cut-throat competition in a bid to claim the Upper Niger.

The British trading company surged forward to create a lead over other European trading companies in the Upper Niger by buying up French and German businesses in the southern part of the Upper Niger, and by applying for a royal charter to negotiate with communities in the Upper Niger. It obtained a royal charter in 1886. This was a common practice—to empower companies to enter into agreements with peoples and polities so that when their respective home countries were strong enough to assert authority, the treaties would be then converted into instruments of sovereignty over the African parties to the treaties.

From then on, not only did the trading company operate illegally by imposing regulations on French and German competitors and by usurping to itself sovereign powers, but it also aggressively signed treaties with over four hundred states and polities in Upper Niger, with the proviso that those communities should not enter into any trade agreements with any French or German companies. Thus the Royal Niger Company combined aggressiveness and illegality in its trade dealings with the Upper Niger communities.

Meanwhile French and German companies sought the backing of their respective governments, but they did so as late starters. The French positioned their troops in Fort Lamie (Bussa) regardless of the treaty the Royal Niger Company had signed at Nikki in 1894. Similarly, the Germans dug in in eastern Benue, especially in Adamawa. There ensued much maneuvering for ascendance, using treaties, commerce, and military force.

By 1898, tension over the Upper Niger between Britain and France on the one hand, and Britain and Germany on the other, reached high fever. The Paris Conference of 1898 was convened to resolve the matter rather than fight inter-European wars on African soil. Bear in mind the irony that through all this, colonization was marketed as a way of ending Africa's intertribal wars. Here were Europeans invading Africa to teach Africans how evil it is to fight one another, about to tear themselves into pieces fighting over Africa in Africa!

At the Paris Conference, the sheer number of treaties that the British company had signed with Upper Niger communities between 1885 and 1898 proved to be the tipping point for France to concede that the Upper Niger was a British sphere of influence. France therefore withdrew its forces from Ft. Lamie (Bussa) in the Upper Niger. The German presence in eastern Benue was the subject of another negotiation later that year.

It was not, however, enough for Britain to invoke sovereignty over the Upper Niger; its sovereign presence also had to be felt. Otherwise, everything was ink on paper and the French were still a threat. Thus Great Britain decided to terminate the Royal Niger Company charter and occupy the Upper Niger as a sovereign nation. This occurred in 1900, and Frederick Lugard—about whom we shall have much to say—was named High Commissioner of the Protectorate of Northern Nigeria.

Note that in order to proclaim the Protectorate of Northern Nigeria, Britain unilaterally tore up over four hundred treaties in Northern Nigeria, in the twinkling of an eye. Lugard had himself participated in the Royal Niger Company's treaty-making mission during 1894–95. Yet neither he, nor Britain, cared to honor contracts made with Nigerian peoples.

Ultimately, then, after much wrangling about names and geographic divisions, there resulted by 1900 three sections: Northern Nigeria Protectorate, with Lugard as High Commissioner; Southern Nigeria Protectorate, with Ralph Moor as High Commissioner; and Lagos and the Yorubaland Protectorate, under Governor William MacGregor. Eventually, and piecemeal, these regions were combined until, in 1914, they were amalgamated to form the single protectorate of Nigeria—under, unfortunately, Frederick Lugard.

Selling Imperialism to the Public

IT WAS one thing for technocrats to do a deal within the four walls of a conference hall; it was another to sell the idea to the electorate. In other words, European nations were faced with the question of making the balkanization of Africa for colonization palatable to their respective electorates, from which soldiers would be recruited for the prospective invasions. Thus the British appropriated the humanitarian slogan used by the London Missionary Society in the eighteenth century: Civilization, Christianity, and Commerce, popularly known as the 3Cs. This came to be called the "white man's burden," a term the poet Rudyard

Kipling coined in 1899.[2] The supposedly superior white man was presented as being morally obligated to raise up the supposedly inferior black man. The Darwinist underpinnings of this notion are clear.

Of course, civilization, Christianity, and commerce all were in place in Africa long before the white man there appeared. Later we will come back to this point; here I wish only to underline the fact that Social Darwinism was used to sell British imperialism to the public, by way of presenting the African as backwards and inferior, in need of the European's help in climbing the evolutionary ladder.

One of the key propagandists involved in this marketing ploy was Flora Lugard, wife of the aforementioned Frederick Lugard. Admittedly, Flora Lugard was not on the administrative staff of Northern Nigeria; nevertheless, her role qualified her as one of the shapers of views, opinions, and decisions in England with great impact on Northern Nigeria. Not only was she the wife of Frederick Lugard, but as a journalist with her own experience in tendentious propaganda, especially during the Boer II war, Flora Lugard performed the unofficial function of a Northern Nigeria Chief Publicist or image maker to the British people. It is she who is credited with suggesting the name "Nigeria" for the British protectorate, in an 1897 article for the London *Times*.

Flora Lugard delivered high-profile lectures in London at the Royal Colonial Institute and at the Royal Society of Arts in 1903 and 1904, respectively. In these lectures she propagated the "Europeans are superior to Africans" ideology, and promoted the idea that Northern Nigeria, which was being administered by her husband, was a territory of superior races as compared to the so-called inferior races of Southern Nigeria. Consider these words: "The pagan races of some very low, some very hardy, types have been driven by native conquerors either towards the coast, where in Southern Nigeria they may been seen in a condition not far removed from the primitive nudity of the forest apes, or into mountain fastnesses."[3] Shortly thereafter she says that the tribes of Nigeria "vary very much among themselves, and the higher types of the Northern states would legitimately protest against a classification which should seem to lower them to the level of the cannibal pagans of the Southern Coast."⁴

Thus she ranks Nigerians on her ladder of evolution, and it should be noted that the cannibalism to which she makes reference has not been proven. At the end of his colonial assignment as Resident (a type of British administrator) of Kabba Province in 1903, Allen Upward stated, "I could not obtain any positive evidence on the subject of cannibalism. But rumour attributed it to the Kukuruku tribes, in whose country Semarika [currently in Edo State] is situated. It was clear to me that the natives either regarded the practice with a certain horror, or had learnt from the Mohammedans and ourselves that it was so regarded by foreigners."⁵

Even Northern Nigerians, however, were sub-human in Flora Lugard's eyes, as the following shall show. In 1905, writing about the rising ascendancy of Japan and the labor shortage facing white Europe, Flora Lugard proposed that Britain harness the African workforce. She softens this baldly self-serving suggestion with a veil of benevolent Social Darwinism: "Our fathers were passionate abolitionists," she writes, "but is it enough that natives in the less-civilised portions of the tropics should have been relieved of the necessity of labouring for others? Is it not desirable that they should take the further step of learning to labour for themselves?" By "for themselves" she means for the British Empire: "The future of native races, and the place which they are to take in the making of the Empire, has rightly been regarded as one of the most interesting that the extension of Empire involves."⁶

To ensure a plentiful labor supply, Flora Lugard advises that the Crown should "put a stop of the practices of slave-raiding and intertribal war" in Northern Nigeria, for these things result in the deaths of able-bodied men and the reduction of a labor force for Britain. She then notes that despite intertribal conflict, "the race is so persistent that it has endured. Let it be preserved with even a moderate amount of care, as elephant and buffalo are in certain regions preserved, and it will increase at a rate which may be a peril or an advantage according to the manner in which it is treated by the white man. It is not difficult to foresee a period when… [the population] of Northern Nigeria may be increased to a total approaching the present total of India."[7]

After thus placing the Northern Nigerian man in the same category as elephants and buffalo, Flora Lugard argues that "if the millions whose increase we have assured by the humanitarian character of our legislation are led to employ themselves in reasonable labour, they will almost necessarily rise in the scale of humanity."[8]

Shortly after these magnanimous remarks, Flora Lugard released her *magnum opus* on Northern Nigeria, the book *A Tropical Dependency*, where she further developed the themes of her lectures and shorter writings, emphasizing how the civilized and benevolent Britain should raise the races of those wretched African colonies from their respective levels of savagery to civilization.[9] Social Darwinian language is prevalent in this book, as for instance when Flora Lugard writes, "Through the whole of the history of these higher races, their tendency has been to drive southwards before them everything that was weak or degraded or outworn. All lower human types to be met with in the country went southwards.…" She then makes plain that these "lower human types" are "the pure negro."[10]

Her husband likewise contributed to the "inferior African" propaganda, as we shall see. I. F. Nicolson writes:

> Volumes could be written about the disastrous results of the success of the Lugards' propaganda; while it would be absurd to claim that they were wholly responsible for such failure as there has been in British administration in Nigeria, or for subsequent political and economic imbalance in the federation, or for the spectacular growth of colour problems and racial prejudice in the twentieth century, their extraordinary version of people and events… has played a terrible part.[11]

Others of course were involved in propagating the "inferior African" narrative, but the Lugards were among the worst offenders.

Flora Lugard versus Constance Larymore

FOR A truer picture of Africans and of the peoples of Northern Nigeria in the early twentieth century, it is imperative to read Constance Larymore's book *A Resident's Wife in Nigeria*,[12] which paints an entirely different picture of Northern Nigeria than did the Lugards.

The Larymores arrived in Northern Nigeria in 1902 and remained for some years. Constance Larymore was a true Christian woman imbued by humanity and truthtelling, who did not attach any significance to her skin color. She frequently speaks highly of those peoples whom she met. For example, Constance Larymore mentions that at Katagun at the edge of the desert, she found a people of "unusual intelligence, coupled with admirable spirit and innate courtesy."[13]

Unlike Flora Lugard, Constance Larymore spent considerable time interacting directly with the people, and did so in a friendly manner. As a result, she liked them and they liked her. Indeed, her friendship with the Sariki earned her a country name. Reflecting on the circumstance years later, she recalled:

> The Sariki explained to me that, as I had evidently been "sent" to them as a special mark of favour, it was quite necessary for them to know my name;—what should they call me? "A man's name," I remarked, "is given to him by his friends. Give me a name yourselves." After cogitating in whispers, the old man said, smiling, that they would in future know me as "Uwamu" (Our Mother), and so I received my "country" name, one that has stuck to me ever since, and by which I am known to all my dark-skinned friends throughout Nigeria. I am always proud of it, for though, at the time, I felt inclined to smile at being so addressed by men old enough to be my father, the title is recognized to be the highest expression of respect and affection that the African man can offer to a woman.[14]

Here is another example of Larymores' difference from the Lugards. At the expiration of Larymore's tenure in Katagun Province, they travelled to Kano on their way back to Zungerum but missed their way and had to pass through Hadeija to get their bearings. On their departure from Hadeija, the emir announced his intention of escorting them on their way as a sign of respect. Furthermore,

> When the last farewells had been said, my husband asked that the Liman might offer prayers for our safe journey, and—perhaps—another

meeting some day, a suggestion which evoked a deep murmur of satis-
faction…. As I turned to mount my pony, the stately old Emir laid his
tender brown hand, with a beautiful amber rosary twined among the
fingers, on my arms, and said gently: "You will come back to us; surely
God will send you back."[15]

Equally instructive is her assessment of some of the memorable
courtesies and friendships among ordinary folks in Kabba, especially the
market women and the traders in the town. She writes:

Of course, it may be called merely superficial friendliness and courtesy,
and it is quite possible that, while the latest arrival absents himself for
ten minutes or so, discoursing to the Resident, the speckled chicken
which erstwhile dangled by one leg and a piece of string from his load
may not be there when he returned, and may be adorning the baggage
of the astute trader, who has just left with some alacrity; but, even so,
for myself, I would gladly take the chance of having my pocket picked,
if, on one of the many occasions when I have entered a crowded omni-
bus in London, one of the row of cold, critical unfriendly faces opposite
would break into a smile, and say what I heard all round me at Kabba,
in sonorous Yoruba: "Akwabo! Akwabo!" (You are welcome, very welcome!)

    Indeed, I can never conquer that curious feeling of chilly depres-
sion that overtakes me each time I return to England, and feel that,
except for the tiny minority of my own friends, I am alone in the crowd;
infinitely more alone in Bond Street, where almost every brick and
stone is familiar, than I could ever be in the busy streets of Kano, or any
other city of Nigeria, which I might enter even for the first time, where
I should find two hands and one willing tongue all inadequate for the
due return of the ceaseless shower of smiling salutations and greetings
that would be poured upon me from every side. And this is by no means
a tribute to any personal charms of mine. Any traveller, black-skinned
or white, receives the same treatment as a matter of course.[16]

Unfortunately, however, the Lugards' presentation of Nigeria pre-
vailed.

Figure 3.1. Lord and Lady Lugard in 1908.

3. British Administrators Echo Darwin

It is important to identify the leading figures in the archi-tectural work of the new protectorate, the personalities whose oppor-tunity it was to administer Northern Nigeria for the Crown. What they had in common was a predisposition to Social Darwinism, the rising ideology of the times. So let us now take a closer look at the men Britain set over Nigeria and see how their language and attitude reflect Darwin's ideas.

Frederick Lugard

We begin as a matter of course with Frederick Lugard, a key figure in the degradation of Nigeria and, moreover, of Africa at large.

Lugard served as High Commissioner of Northern Nigeria from 1900–06, then was sent to Hong Kong as Governor, and then returned as Governor-General of both the Southern Nigeria Protectorate and the Northern Nigerian Protectorate from 1912–19. During that time, in 1914, the Southern Nigeria Protectorate and the Northern Nigeria Pro-tectorate were amalgamated as the Colony and Protectorate of Nigeria, under Lugard as Governor.

In 1905 Lugard contributed a chapter on West Africa to a book titled *The Empire and the Century*. In it he refers in decidedly Darwinian terms to the "native races, who are centuries behind ourselves in mental evolution" and should be "gradually brought to a higher plane of civili-sation and progress."[1] Further, he professed himself "confident that the genius of our race will be among the first to recognize the growing, and, indeed, already vital, importance to civilisation of the raw products of the tropics, with the necessity for organizing the industry of its teeming millions and promoting their welfare."[2] Thus Lugard clearly reveals the goal—obtaining possession of Africa's wealth—covered with a mere fig leaf of concern for the supposedly less-evolved races.

In 1922 Lugard wrote a book titled *The Dual Mandate in British Tropical Africa*, which strongly influenced not only subsequent British administrators in Nigeria, but British policies in Africa at large. W. R. Crocker, who served as an administrator in Nigeria in the early 1930s, wrote of Lugard's book, "To praise it would be an impertinence. There is nothing else quite like it in all the literature of British imperialism."[3] He says this because Lugard popularized the pre-existing strategy of Indirect Rule, a policy by which colonizers governed through local rulers.

Crocker summarizes *The Dual Mandate* and its influence thus:

> Africa, so the argument ran, could not be left shut up merely for the benefit of the African; the outside world also had an interest in and a claim to share its great and special kind of wealth; but the outside world, in exercising its legitimate claim, must heed the legitimate interests of the African and must therefore comport itself as his trustee. Obligations, like interests, were dual.
>
> As an example of how the outside world should exercise its trusteeship, details were set out of the system of administration that had been built up in Northern Nigeria, which was described as Indirect Rule. The book came at an opportune time.... The British conscience was becoming more and more sensitive about the Empire. The Dual Mandate was a comforting as well as a highly informative book. Lord Lugard's fame and the success of his book put Nigeria on the map.[4]

Put Nigeria on the map? Most clearly, Lugard's view of Nigeria and of the African had far-reaching impact on how others viewed and treated the African. His view is summed up by these statements: "The civilised Powers of the world have asserted the unequivocal right and obligation of the more advanced races to assume responsibility for the backward races,"[5] and "We hold these countries because it is the genius of our race to colonise, to trade, and to govern."[6] In this way, as I. F. Nicolson notes, "he lets the real, true imperialist cat out of the bag."[7]

Further, Lugard claims that "the subject races of Africa are not yet able to stand alone."[8] This remark is particularly ironic, for no nation on earth has the capability of standing alone, whether economically, politically, socially, culturally, or otherwise. If Europe were able to stand alone, why was there such a scramble for Africa up to the point that Britain and France on the one hand, and Britain and Germany on the other hand, stood on the verge of going to war on and in Africa? It was simply because they could not stand alone economically without Africa.

Lugard punctuates his narrative with condescending appellations throughout, clearly indicating that he considers the African to be less advanced than the European. For example, Lugard describes the Lagos Colony as including "many who are still in the lowest stage of primitive savagery."[9]

Note the language Lugard uses in this heavily derogatory passage:

> Such in brief are the peoples for whose welfare we are responsible in British tropical Africa. They have a fascination of their own, for we are dealing with the child races of the world, and learning at first hand the habits and customs of primitive man; a virile and expanding race whose men are often models of symmetry and strength—a race which illustrates every stage in the evolution of human society, from the hardly human bushman of the Kalahari and the lowest type of cannibal, to the organised despotism and barbaric display of a negro kingdom like that of Uganda as we found it, where royalty is hedged about with more observance than in a modern palace in Europe.[10]

Child races? The hardly human bushman? Every stage in the evolution of human society? In Lugard's Darwinian view there are advanced races, which are white European; and there are backwards races, which are black African.

We will turn later to the question of whether these "primitive" peoples were truly as backwards and barbaric as Lugard claims. Here, we focus attention on the incontestable fact that Lugard echoes and propagates Darwin's notion that some peoples are more highly evolved than others.

Further, in Darwinian manner Lugard divides Africa into differing "races" and spells out his belief that the larger the amount of negroid blood, the more inferior the race. He writes, "All have been modified to a greater or less degree by admixture with negro blood, which has produced racial types differing from each other, and widely different from the negro type. They vary in their mental and physical characteristics according to the amount of negro blood in their veins, which has shown itself extremely potent in assimilating alien strains to its own type."[11]

Lugard refers to the lighter-skinned peoples as Hamites (Fulani are included in this) and opines that "they exhibit... powers of organisation and intellectual development in advance of the pure negro stock. They are capable of immense physical endurance, but do not possess the physique and strength of the negroes."[12]

As for the more negroid, Lugard wrote in true Darwinist fashion that they are closer to animals than are white men:

> The Bantus, and most other negros, are physically fine specimens of the human race. Powerfully built, they are capable of great feats of strength and endurance.... In character and temperament the typical African of this race-type is a happy, thriftless, excitable person, lacking in self-control, discipline, and foresight, naturally courageous, and naturally courteous and polite, full of personal vanity, with little sense of veracity, fond of music, and "loving weapons as an oriental loves jewelry." His thoughts are concentrated on the events and feelings of the moment, and he suffers little from apprehension for the future, or grief for the past. "His mind," says Sir C. Eliot, "is far nearer to the animal world than that of the European or Asiatic, and exhibits something of the animal's placidity and want of desire to rise beyond the state he has reached."[13]

Lugard here is quoting Sir Charles Eliot, who served as Commissioner of British East Africa from 1900–04.[14] Eliot in his own book, leading up to his Darwinian pronouncement that Africans are closer to animals than are Europeans or Asians, writes:

Figure 3.2. Sir Charles Eliot, Commissioner of British East Africa.

Quick excitability is the chief mental characteristic of Africans. They are dominated by the transient emotion or impulse of the moment, and neither remember what has preceded, nor look forward to what is likely to follow.... [He is] incapable of self-restraint, foresight, and fixed purpose or organisation.... The African is greedy and covetous... but he is too indolent in his ways, and too disconnected in his ideas, to make any attempt to better himself, or to undertake any labour which does not produce a speedy and visible result.[15]

After quoting Eliot, Lugard continues in insulting vein:

He lacks power of organisation, and is conspicuously deficient in the management and control alike of men or of business. He loves the display of power, but fails to realise its responsibility. His most universal natural ability lies in eloquence and oratory. He is by no means lacking in industry and will work hard with a less incentive than most races. He has the courage of the fighting animal—an instinct rather than a moral virtue. He is very prone to imitate anything new in dress or custom, whether it be the turban and flowing gown of the Moslem, or the straw hat and trousers of the European, however unsuited to his environment and conditions of life. He is an apt pupil, and a faithful and devoted friend.

In brief, the virtues and the defects of this race-type are those of attractive children, whose confidence when once it has been won is given ungrudgingly as to an older and wiser superior, without question and without envy....

Perhaps the two traits which have impressed me as those most characteristic of the African native are his lack of apprehension and inability to visualise the future, and the steadfastness of his loyalty and affection.[16]

The disparagements are plentiful, and even the compliments sting. Notice that "he is an apt pupil" is a restatement and an echo of a core assumption of Social Darwinism, a justification of the "Europeans are superior to Africans" propaganda. And, as an aside, I would ask whether proclivity to imitate new fashion in Africa is distinguishable from that of the catwalk epicenters in London and Paris.

And so we see that a key and highly influential British administrator embraced Darwin's evolutionary view of the superior, civilized white man and the inferior, barbaric black.

If his own words are not evidence enough of Lugard's debt to Darwin, witness also Lugard's admiration for the Social Darwinist Karl Pearson.

Pearson, an arch-eugenicist, firmly believed not only that natural selection—the survival of the fittest—applied to humans, but that humans should actively seek to apply its principles. He wrote:

A community of men is as subject as a community of ants or as a herd of buffaloes to the laws which rule all organic nature. We cannot escape from them; it serves no purpose to protest at what some may call their cruelty and their bloodthirstiness. We can only study these laws, recognise what of gain they have brought to man, and urge the statesman and the thinker to regard and use them.[17]

Pearson elevated the action of natural selection to the level of whole nations and presented his view as "the scientific view of a nation,"[18] in which he justified war against "inferior races" as a logical implication of

Darwin's theory of evolution, and for which he promoted his National Efficiency socio-political program.

In brief, Pearson defines a nation as "an organized whole, kept up to a high pitch of internal efficiency by ensuring that its numbers are substantially recruited from the better stocks, and kept up to a high pitch of external efficiency by contest, chiefly by way of war with inferior races, and with equal races by the struggle for trade-routes and for the sources of raw material and of food supply."[19]

Pearson says, further, "The path of progress is strewn with the wrecks of nations; traces are everywhere to be seen of the hecatombs of inferior races, and of victims who found not the narrow way to perfection. Yet these dead people are, in very truth, the stepping-stones on which mankind has arisen to the higher intellectual and deeper emotional life of today."[20]

It is not insignificant that Lugard found a way of quoting Pearson approvingly in the second page of the first chapter of his 643-page *Dual Mandate*, saying that during the Scramble for Africa, "the instinct of the nation [Britain] recognised with Dr. Pearson that 'the permanency of Empire consists in its extension.'"[21] It stands to reason therefore to suggest that Pearson's thought was certainly pivotal in shaping governance in colonial Northern Nigeria.

Benjamin Kidd was another significant personality that Lugard respected immensely vis-à-vis governance in Northern Nigeria. A Social Darwinist also of the eugenics variety, Kidd endorsed the erroneous analogy between the evolution of biological organisms and human society. A prolific writer, Kidd travelled extensively throughout America, Canada, and Africa between 1898 and 1902, with those travels resulting in a series of articles commissioned by the *Times* of London, and later published under the title *The Control of the Tropics* in 1898. The sequel, *The Principles of Western Civilisation*, was published in 1902, propounding Kidd's racist teaching that the English are a superior race—and contradicting himself in the process, for it is illogical to believe both that white race intellectual superiority is due to accumulated knowledge, and

PRINCIPLES OF WESTERN CIVILISATION

BEING THE FIRST VOLUME OF A SYSTEM OF EVOLUTIONARY PHILOSOPHY

Figure 3.3. Social Darwinist Benjamin Kidd promoted an evolutionary account of human development in his book *The Principles of Western Civilisation* (1902).

also to attribute the supposed superiority to Darwinian innate endowment.[22]

However, Kidd underwent a change of heart when World War I was looming and he was forced to admit that, instead of human beings evolving beyond wars, alas, human beings were degenerating further into bloodshed. This to Kidd was an unsustainable contradiction. Hence, he not only threw out of the window his earlier Social Darwinist beliefs, but he also indicted the unilinear view of human society, imperialism, and the vaunting glories of Western civilization.[23]

Lugard, however, in 1921 knowingly quoted repeatedly from Kidd's *The Control of the Tropics* of 1898 and referenced Kidd's articles in the *Times* of those days in order to shore up his various spurious arguments—years after Kidd had denounced his earlier beliefs in Social Darwinism. Lugard, for example, cites Kidd: "There never has been, and never will be within any time with which we are practically concerned, such a thing as good government in the European sense of the tropics by the natives of these regions."[24] Also: "'The tropics will never be developed by the natives themselves,' says Kidd…. The development must be under British guidance."[25]

The Social Darwinist attitude evidenced by Lugard in his book is also apparent in his annual reports to British Parliament. The following are sample phrases taken from the 1900–1901 report: "negroid tribes," "pagan tribes, without cohesion," "wholly uncivilised pagan tribes."[26] In Lugard's 1902 report he refers to "the African savage in his primitive state [who] can understand nothing but force," "truculent tribes," "lawless pagan tribes," and "wild pagan tribes."[27] In 1903 he refers to Bassa-region Northern Nigerians as "mere savages" and "untutored savages" (who nevertheless show "much ingenuity in smuggling gin from Southern Nigeria"), and "warlike pagan tribes."[28] In Lugard's 1904 report he continues to refer to "pagan tribes," "uncivilised and savage tribes," and "primitive peoples," adding in this report that many are cannibals (which was not proven) and mentioning the "inferior negroid races" driven south by lighter-skinned groups.[29] And so forth in his other reports.

Charles Temple

ANOTHER BRITISH administrator who echoed Darwin's ideas was Charles Lindsay Temple, Lieutenant Governor of Northern Nigeria from 1914 until 1917.

Charles Temple had strong Social Darwinist views. For Temple the Nigerian population was a teeming mass of what he called native races. In his book, *Native Races and Their Rulers*, which he completed a year after early retirement from Northern Nigeria, he used the terms "native races" twenty-nine times, and "native subject races" seven times in his description of Nigerians.

Temple wrote that the native is in "a different stage of development to ourselves."[30] The peoples of Western Europe "have been so favoured by Providence" that they "occupy today a dominating position among the races of the world," and "among these nations none has probably been so favoured as Great Britain."[31]

Some pages later he elaborates on the supposed differences between the British and the "native":

The native is a human being like ourselves, but in a different stage of development. Some natives are, even to-day, in the stage of our Druidical ancestors, whereas others are in the stage which we passed through in about the Middle Ages. The whirligig of time has brought us from five hundred to a thousand years ahead of them in the process of evolution, that is all.[32]

He then goes on to ever-so-generously note, "We do not know what happened in the obscure past; who will dare to prophecy what will happen in the obscure future? Which of the races now existing on the earth will be found to be the ruling races 5,000 years hence. It well may happen that some dark-skinned writer... will coin happy phrases descriptive of the white races, who knows?" But for now, he writes, "It is our great privilege and our great responsibility... to control the development of literally hundreds of millions of human beings, which constitute the native subject races."[33]

Ordained by the forces of evolution, since Northern Nigerian peoples were at a lower stage of development than the British, and the British were the most favored by the evolutionary imperative, "the destiny of nations," Temple says, "has placed under our control... so great a teeming mass of dusky humanity that history furnishes no parallel."[34]

Tellingly, after beating the drum of Britain's noble responsibility, he notes that the white man's "very existence as a distinct race" rides on the outcome.[35] He hoped to find a way "so that the native subject races may remain in existence, unfused with ours, and yet in subjection." The analogy he then makes is of "a more competent man and a less competent, by virtue of which the more competent can control the actions of the less competent for the advantage of both."[36]

And how to control the native? Temple here makes recourse to the cloaking language of benevolence. "We can truly assist the development of the native under our care," Temple writes.

That path follows the natural evolution of the native race. We must lead him along that path, and not persuade or compel him to leave it and follow our path.... We may... give him, in very limited numbers, the keys of learning, of art, of science. But what are all these things compared to fellowship, companionship, the society of equals, pride of race, patriotism? Of these great essentials we deprive him when we persuade him to leave the fellowship of his kind, the frame in which Providence has set him, and to enter within the pale of our society where he must be as a stranger at the feast.[37]

Hence, Temple supported segregation and Indirect Rule, with an intermediary (as we shall see, a lighter-skinned native) between the black native and the white ruler.

One cannot but share Christopher Alderman's observation that "the techniques which Temple proposed for interpreting specific native customs, beliefs and institutions, as well as his version of the policy of Indirect Rule, displayed Social Darwinist assumptions.... Temple not only used Social Darwinism to explain racial differences and justify British imperialism, but also caused it to have a direct impact on the practical administration of colonial rule in Northern Nigeria."[38]

Against the Tide

IT SHOULD be noted that a few British administrators swam against the tide of racist Social Darwinism thought. G. W. Webster, Resident in Sokoto, had to decide whether to continue to stand with pernicious racist beliefs or stand with his heart. He eventually decided to follow his heart and married a Nigerian. So infuriated was Lugard that he urged that Webster "should be cleared out at once."[39]

Likewise Resident H. Edwardes lost his job because he crossed the racist line between Europeans and Africans. While that was not insignificant to the establishment, the greater danger he posed was his refusal to conceal financial impropriety wherever it was found, contrary to the wishes of the powers that be, which wanted disclosure of corruption to be selective. This is a man who "thought deeply about why he was in Africa and what his obligations to the Africans were,"[40] hence "he was notoriously a friend of the peasants."[41] For Edwardes, "The best way of keeping in touch with ordinary people was to sleep at some distance from the rest of his party when touring, thus making it possible for peasants to approach him at night with their complaints, unseen by messengers, emir's representatives, and servants, the bureaucratic and social outer wrapping that insulated many officers from the masses."[42]

"Profoundly interested in education [with] well developed ideas on Africa's future,"[43] Edwardes engaged in "vigorous public works, such as irrigation and road building, on a scale that was impressive for the 1920s."[44] Rather than rewarding Edwardes, the other Residents saw him as a threat and a traitor to the status quo. The last straw that saw him out of Northern Nigeria may not have been unconnected with his undisguised humanity with the people, whose affairs he presided over. Against the grain of the "Europeans are superior to African" ethos, Edwardes committed the unpardonable administrative offence of referring to the people of Bauchi Province as "my people."[45] As far as the authorities at the top were concerned, Edwardes had crossed the line—the imaginary organic chasm between Europeans and Africans—and that alone constituted "the point of no return."[46] He was sacked.

A few other exceptions in Northern Nigeria shall be mentioned later. Also, for clarity's sake, let it be noted that other areas of Nigeria fared far better than did Northern Nigeria because their British administrators did not cling to Social Darwinist notions of humanity. Recall that the Southern Nigeria Protectorate had Ralph Moor as High Commissioner, and Lagos and the Yorubaland Protectorate had William MacGregor. Both MacGregor and Moor "had great respect for the people they governed.... MacGregor in particular had taken pains to refute the idea of Negro inferiority."[47]

Lugard deliberately distanced himself from MacGregor and the Lagos administration because the two were oriented towards two different goals. Whereas MacGregor was working towards the advancement of the people of his colony—for example, by 1906 medical research was underway in Lagos that would result in a Nobel Prize—Frederick Lugard was scheming the unmitigated exploitation and dehumanization of the people of Northern Nigeria.

Moreover, Governor MacGregor mounted the podium at the Royal African Society meeting in London to deliver a lecture entitled, "Lagos, Abeokuta and Alake." His lecture was an apparent rebuttal to the pre-

Figure 3.4. Sir William MacGregor, Governor of Lagos Protectorate, Nigeria, from 1899–1904.

viously mentioned speech delivered by Flora Lugard. Among other re-marks, MacGregor said:

> In point of character the Yoruba negro is a very interesting study. What at first sight strikes one most forcibly is the courtesy of the chiefs and people. Taken as a body, the chiefs of Yorubaland might serve as a model of politeness to any people in Europe. This pleasing quality is not confined to the upper classes, for it is very strongly marked in the children, and among the very poorest of the market women.
>
> The second quality that distinguishes the Yoruba is his patriotism. No race of men could be more devoted to their country. All the princi-pal chiefs are clearly opposed to such hideous things as the slave mar-ket, human sacrifice, cruel punishment, and gross oppression of any kind or form.[48]

McGregor further noted that "the Yoruba has as clear ideas as to the rights of property as Englishmen have" and that Sir Ralph Moor "enter-tains a high opinion of the capability of the Yoruba soldier." He also said:

> It is difficult for one that knows the Yoruba race to believe that in point of intellectual capacity they are inferior to Europeans.... A consider-

able number of native ladies and gentlemen have been well educated at home and in this country [courtesy of Christian missions], and are quite fit to be put on social equality with any Europeans in the colony; several natives practise successfully as doctors and lawyers; a considerable number are clergymen; and there are many natives high in the Civil Service.... They are very strongly conservative, and cling with tenacity to old ways and usages; but an excellent proof was given last year of the fact that they can warmly embrace a new idea.[49]

MacGregor thus painted a wholly different picture than did the Lugards, one that does not conform so conveniently to the Social Darwinist notion of inferior races.

When the architects of British administration in Northern Nigeria are, as we have seen, thorough Social Darwinists, can it be any wonder that they imposed upon Northern Nigeria a method of governance steeped in Social Darwinism? Let us look now at specific effects of the Social Darwinist attitude on the Northern Nigeria administration.

tency of each. In like manner we may follow backward the ancestral line of the anthropoids until we find it converging with the line representing the lemuroids or the carnivores, or both. We thus see the lines of the higher animal life coming together at some point in the remote past, at which time the ancestry of all these forms existed in a common type from which divergence, first into varie- and unmistakable indications of science the whole vertebrate kingdom of organic forms approximating at the last to a common type. This is to say that a single ancestry of a given but unknown form at one time contained the potency and elements of all the multifarious developments which have since taken place in the widely distributed and greatly divergent vertebrate animals of the earth

PROGRESSIVE DEVELOPMENT OF MAN.—(2) EVOLUTION ILLUSTRATED WITH THE SIX CORRESPONDING LIVING FORMS.

Figure 4.1. Racist chart from 1912 depicting the "progressive development" of human races. Blacks are depicted as the races closest to ape-like creatures.

4. The Evolutionary Ladder

Accorded to Frederick Lugard's biographer, Margery Perham, Indirect Rule as advocated by Lugard is the colonial system of government by which colonial authorities empower existing potentates with local structures and traditions to exercise authority over their people with colonial officials ensuring compliance for the achievement of the colonial objectives.[1]

Indirect Rule can be made to sound quite reasonable in that it utilizes native rulers and seeks to disrupt native customs as little as possible. However, in the case of Northern Nigeria, condescension and racism were behind Lugard's push for this method. As Erik Gilbert and Jonathan T. Reynolds note, "Influenced by scientific racism and social Darwinism... Lugard advocated the use of existing African political systems in no small part because he believed the complexity of European culture was simply unsuitable for the 'African mind.'"[2]

Who Rules in Indirect Rule?

One issue that naturally arises in the framework of Indirect Rule is that of who the intermediary rulers should be. The wisest and most moral local people? Those who are respected and trusted? Lugard claimed that he chose his intermediaries—the Islamic Fulani—because they were already rulers, and because their beliefs reflected that of the majority of the people, but neither of those assertions is true.

First, the region was not uniformly Muslim. Christians and pagans populated the area as well. It is a fact that there were more pagans than

Muslims in Northern Nigeria in 1900. There was no such thing as the Islamic nature of the Northern way of life and institutions because the land and peoples comprising Northern Nigeria were pluralist, with pagans in the majority.

As for reflecting the beliefs of the majority of the people, that is not true either. Pagans with their animistic religious beliefs were in many ways more civilized than Muslims. Consider that in African traditional societies, for a man to put away his wife is regarded as a proof of immaturity and sheer irresponsibility, for which his peers or his clan can fine him or place him under discipline, making it difficult for him to get another wife in the same community. The same thing applies to a wife. In contrast, in Muslim societies, a man can divorce his wife by declaring, "I divorce you" to her face three times—a requirement that can take less than ten seconds. There is also a procedure, albeit over a longer period, for a wife to divorce her husband.

It is furthermore a fact that venereal disease was unknown among the Tangale of Gombe East until around 1928 after colonial rule had exposed them to Muslims from the northern direction.[3] (Indeed, venereal disease was known "as the 'white man's disease' for it is said that it was the white man who brought syphilis to Africa.")[4] And it was on account of the treatment of Muslim women in Northern Nigeria that Ethel Miller, an English woman missionary, wrote a pamphlet title *Women Count* in 1926. Therefore let us be clear that Islam wins no points on the civilization scale, nor did it reflect the values of the majority population.

As for the colonizers' other excuse, that the Fulani were already in positions of power, it must be noted that on those occasions when the Fulani were in power they were not good rulers, nor were they popular. These Fulani were latecomers to Africa, cattle nomads with no homeland of their own. They conquered certain regions during the Fula jihads of the eighteenth and nineteenth centuries, engaging heavily in slavery and trafficking in violence. The ultimate result was the Sokoto Caliphate, led by Dan Fodio. The only reason why the Fulani defeated the pagan armies was because the Fulani had horses and the pagans had no horses. The pagans could not sustain horse bases because of the terrain. Of course, the pagans resisted the annual raids and cursed them!

Indeed, if tolerance is a mark of the stage of development along the contrived evolutionary ladder, then pagan African religion is far ahead of Islam because African religion is characterized by worship-your-God-and-I-worship-mine. The old Benin Kingdom, which was brought to its knees in December 1897, is perhaps most illustrative of this point, as virtually every household catered for its own shrine. There is no proselytization in African primal religions, unlike what is historically verifiable—a trail of fire and the sword in the wake of Islamic jihads, especially in Northern Nigeria throughout the nineteenth century.

The missionary Walter Miller noted that typical Fulani traits of "a naturally cruel and vindictive nature, have made them tyrants rather than rulers"[5] and "these Fulani rulers... enjoy the pain of their people."[6] Miller gives explicit details of horrific torture imposed by the Fulani. Fulani rule was an example of a multi-dimensional hydra-headed monstrosity, and its Fulani functionaries were precipitators, prosecutors, and perpetuators of dehumanization which knew no bounds.

In governance and taxation they were also unfair. As Chinedu Ubah notes, "As a result of bribery, high-handedness and corruption in the system, the peasants felt oppressed."[7]

Indeed at one point Lugard himself admits what was known to Christian mission agencies long before 1900, but which Lugard preferred to disregard:

> The Fulani never thoroughly conquered the country, and succeeded only in gaining the submission of the great towns in the plains where their horsemen were effective. The pagan tribes in the hills and broken country and even in large areas of the plains maintained their independence. They were constantly raided for slaves and retaliated by attacking caravans and frequently carried the war up to the gates of the Fulani walled towns.[8]

He says further that "the Fulani rule, in fact, had never... been fully accepted, even in the Kano Province, the very heart of Hausaland, and the Emir stated that the peasantry had always been truculent and rebellious, and that it had been necessary for the Emirs to tour round their country annually, with all their forces, to ensure the payment of taxes."[9] Thus Northern Nigeria was not predominantly Muslim, nor were the Fulani good or popular rulers, nor were they rulers everywhere.

From 1900–1903, Lugard's force advanced northwards to occupy Northern Nigeria, moving through mostly pagan polities who had never bowed to Islam. For example, Lugard refers to "a series of towns"[10] between Zaria and Kano. That is a reference to the Maguzawa—pagan Hausa in Hausa heartland—who have never bowed to Islam throughout their history up to the twenty-first century. These people "remained quietly in their towns and brought ample supplies of food and water for the troops."[11] Why did they support Lugard's troops? Because they believed that the advancing force was coming out to liberate them from the jihadists. To their utter shock, Frederick Lugard did the opposite by re-imposing Fulani rulers.

Why, then, did Lugard choose the Islamic Fulani? Why choose the brutal, unpopular, minority Fulani to act as intermediaries between the British and the rest of the population? There were three religions in the region. Since primal religion had no chance of competing, one would have expected Lugard to list the strengths of Christianity on one side and the strengths of Islam on the other side for comparison and make the choice transparent and accountable. Instead he chose Islam, and for reasons that, as we have seen, were not good reasons at all but were mere excuses.

Darwinian Racism

THE FULANI had, in Lugard's mind, one dominant advantage: They were lighter of skin and therefore, in Lugard and his colleagues' minds, of more advanced evolutionary status.

This is well documented by Lugard's own words. Lugard referred to the lighter-skinned peoples as Hamites (Fulani are included in this) and claimed that "they exhibit... powers of organisation and intellectual development in advance of the pure negro stock."[12] In Lugard's 1900–1901 report to Parliament, he notes, "The Fulani rule has been maintained as an experiment, for I am… anxious to utilize, if possible, their wonderful intelligence, for they are born rulers, and incomparably above the negroid tribes in ability."[13] He further wrote that "the Fulani of Norther Nigeria are, as I have said, more capable of rule than the indigenous races,"[14] and further that "such races form an invaluable medium between the British staff and the native peasantry. Nor can the difficulty of finding any one capable of taking their place, or the danger they would constitute to the State if ousted from their positions, be ignored. Their traditions of rule, their monotheistic religion, and their intelligence enable them to appreciate more readily than the negro population the wider objects of British policy."[15]

In Lugard's opinion, then, the fairer-skinned Fulani were evolutionarily superior to the "negro population" or "negroid tribes."

Likewise his wife, Flora, giving a lecture on March 1, 1904, at a meeting of the Royal Society of Arts in London, opined:

> We may roughly divide the population of Nigeria into three parts: There are Fulani, who are the military and the ruling class, fast falling into a degradation by the vices which are apt to undermine the despotism of uncurbed power but still representing authority as which has existed in the eyes of three or four generations. There are the Hausas, once themselves the ruling class and now representing the industry, the agriculture and the commerce of the country. And below these are the tribes too numerous to catalogue.[16]

Flora Lugard wrote that the Fulani "count as a partly white race," and that "the Haussa and the Songhay are other races [in addition to Fulani] which, though black, are absolutely distinct from the pure negro type."[17] Of "the Songhay race" she writes that "their skin is black like the negro, but there is otherwise nothing negroid in their appearance." She then goes on to describe their thin lips, their noses which are not flat, and so forth.[18]

She speaks of the Fulani as "a striking people, dark in complexion, having doubtless intermarried with negro races, but of the distinguished features, small hands and fine, rather aristocratic carriage of the Arabs as we know them on the Mediterranean coast. They are of the Mohammedan religion, and are held by those who know them to be naturally endowed with the characteristics which fit them for rule."[19] She elsewhere describes the Fulani as "tawny," and waxes eloquent regarding their intelligence, importance, and "aristocracy."[20]

Indeed, she says of the Fulani, "We seem to be in the presence of one of the great fundamental facts of history that there are races which are born to conquer and others to persist under conquest."[21] This is an assertion steeped in Social Darwinism, as is her remark that in Northern Nigeria, "every white man is in a position of authority, and every white man owes it to himself and his country to maintain the dignity of the place in which he finds himself."[22]

Given the Lugards' ranking of Fulani first, Hausa second, and all others last, it is a matter of extreme incongruity that Lugard did not recruit a single Fulani man to join his elite bodyguards. Rather, the approximately seventy of them were exclusively Yoruba—dark-skinned men from the despised south. In other words, when the chips were down, it was only among the Yoruba that Frederick Lugard could lie down and close both eyes. How ironic, that the Yoruba from whom Lugard drew his most trusted guards were "savages"—indeed, were savages in the group deemed by his wife to be cannibals!

The Lugards were not alone in elevating the Fulani on the basis of skin color. In Britain at the Home Office, administrators were all too ready to take "the assessment by Lugard of Fulani superiority as axiomatic, revealed truth."[23] Fulani superiority "was not a new myth, for Europeans had long been fascinated by the mystery of the origin of the Fulani; the lightness of their skin was doubtless enough to suggest some kind of inherent superiority, to those conditioned to react in such a way."[24]

In Northern Nigeria, other British administrators who had a strong view on the superiority of the Fulani included Charles Orr, a political officer at the territorial headquarters in Zungeru. For example, Orr claimed:

> The Fulanis, known also as Fellata, Fulahs, Pulbe, Puls, and by various synonyms, are unquestionably the most remarkable and interesting of all the tribes and nations of Equatorial Africa. Their origin is as obscure as that of the Hausa, but they differ fundamentally from the latter in almost every particular. The true Fulani is not negroid. His complexion is fair, his features regular, his hair long and straight.... Fulanis have always kept aloof from other races, and have looked upon themselves as a "white race," infinitely superior to the negro. Their pride of race has been justified.[25]

Charles Temple also put the Fulani higher on the evolutionary ladder. Temple was a rising influence in the Colonial Office, and among his colleagues in Northern Nigeria, most especially at the time he expressed this opinion.[26] While Flora Lugard divides the Nigerian population into three, representing the supposed respective evolutionary levels of each, Temple makes geography a specific element and divides the Northern Nigerian population into three regions of "teeming millions of natives of many races."[27] Just as Flora places the Fulani at the head of the population, Temple accords the Fulani the first place in the order of evolutionary hierarchy.[28]

There is no doubt, however, that to Temple and the Lugards even the Fulani were far lower than the white man. Temple saw such a chasm between white and black that he declares "fusion between the European and the dark-skinned races of Africa is entirely out of the question." He then speaks at length of the evils of intermarriage.[29]

Lugard, too, emphasizes the chasm between the British and the Fulani:

> The Fulani of Northern Nigeria are, as I have said, more capable of rule than the indigenous races, but in proportion as we consider them an alien race, we are denying self-government to the people over whom they rule, and supporting an alien caste—albeit closer and more akin

to the native races than a European can be. Yet capable as they are, it requires the ceaseless vigilance of the British staff to maintain a high standard of administrative integrity, and to prevent oppression of the peasantry.[30]

In a report designed to elevate her husband's work, Flora Lugard says in patronizing manner, "In consequence of the cordial cooperation and remarkable administrative aptitudes of the Fulani, when they once understand that oppression and tyranny are forbidden, the work of the provinces is being carried on with a smaller number of white men than might have been imagined possible."[31]

Thus the Lugards, and others, can sometimes be found elevating the Fulani and sometimes denigrating them, always in aid of codifying the ladder of evolutionary progress.

WEST AFRICA PAYS A VISIT TO ENGLAND

Figure 5.1. The Islamic Emir of Katsena from Northern Nigeria on his visit to England in 1921.

5. ELEVATING ISLAM

IN HIS PRAISE FOR THE FULANI, FREDERICK LUGARD NOTED THAT they "for the most part have embraced Islam."[1] Flora Lugard predicted that further research would show a correlation between race and religion. In her view, the "pure negro" was lower than the lighter-skinned "finer races" who embraced Islam.[2]

Islam vs Paganism

IN LUGARD'S 1904 report to Parliament he refers to "inferior negroid races" who were driven south by "the great civilised empires of Songhay"[3]—Songhay being Islamic. Likewise Flora Lugard designates a geographical region where the "debased pagan negro" lives, as compared to a region of greater civilization where "the finer black races"—the "Mussulman" or Muslim races—live.[4]

Frederick Lugard writes:

For the most part the progressive communities adopted, and owed their advance to the adoption of, an alien monotheistic religion, which brought with it a written language and a foreign culture. It is to the creed of Islam that this political and social influence has in the past alone been due. It has been the more potent as a creative and regenerating force, because it brought with it an admixture of Aryan or Hamitic blood... they possessed greater powers of social organisation than the negro aborigines, and may therefore claim to be of a superior race-type.

.... The modern history of the advanced communities of Hausaland and Bornu in Nigeria "may be said to date from the period at which they accepted the Moslem religion, though the purer black races established their domination over the inferior, and ruled by force of superior intelligence and cultivation long before that time." ... Their descendants, the Fulani, still form the dominant caste, and rule the Moslem states of Nigeria.[5]

Thus Lugard demonstrates his belief that only more highly evolved Africans accepted Islam.

He acknowledges that "by supporting [Fulani] rule we unavoidably encourage the spread of Islam, which from the purely administrative point of view has the disadvantage of being subject to waves of fanaticism."[6]

However, he assures his readers that it matters little: "As a religion it does not evoke in the pure negro the ardent zeal which it excites in the races of alien or mixed blood, and there is often little to differentiate the peasant or labourer who calls himself a Mahomedan from his pagan brother."[7]

Again, however, Lugard makes it clear that even "advanced" Africans are far below white Europeans. He writes, "Mr. Bosworth-Smith shows that [Islam] is a religion incapable of the highest development, but its limitations suit the limitations of the people. It has undeniably had a civilising effect, abolishing the gross forms of pagan superstition and barbarous practices, and adding to the dignity, self-respect, and self-control of its adherents."[8]

W. R. Crocker, who worked in the British Colonial Service in Nigeria, likewise noted, "The great merit of Islam is that it offers the African an explanation of the Universe and a code of ethics superior to his own and yet not too difficult or too different from his own."[9]

Islam vs Christianity

CHRISTIANITY WAS conceived as too difficult for the black man to grasp or to follow.

Lugard wrote of Christianity that "its more abstruse tenets, its stricter code of sexual morality, its exaltation of peace and humility, its recognition of brotherhood with the slave, the captive, and the criminal, do not altogether appeal to the temperament of the negro."[10] Islam was, he felt, a better fit than Christianity for the violent and intellectually limited black man:

> Islam as a militant creed which teaches contempt for those who are not its votaries, panders to the weakness of the African character—self-conceit and vanity. Centuries of lawless strife have made the African a worshipper of force, and he has been quick to adopt the creed of the conqueror, chiefly for the prestige it brought. Its very excesses, the capture of women as slaves and concubines, and the looting of villages, though hateful enough when he is himself the victim, form the beau ideal of his desires if he can be the aggressor.
>
> And there is much else which appeals to the African and suits his conditions, in the religion of Mahomet. It sanctions polygamy, which is natural to the tropics.... It has the attraction of an indigenous religion spread by the people themselves, or by men of like race with similar social standards.[11]

Like Lugard, Crocker thought Islam suitable for the Nigerian. He writes, "The more completely Christianity is apprehended, on the other hand, the more completely does it separate the African from his old natural way of life and from his natural environment.... Even the propagators of Islam are men of his own race, often of his own village." Crocker continues, "It is not merely that... [the Moslem's] religion is free of the vulgarity of most Christian converts with their execrable Moody and Sankey hymn tunes and crude texts, but the Moslem has a poise and a stability and a code which the Christian convert generally (by no means always) lacks; probably because the Moslem can practice something he can understand, while the Christian convert cannot. Thus, as I see it, Islam is a religion better suited to Africa."[12]

Though Crocker insults the aesthetics of Western hymns, he later also disparages those very missionaries who expressed a desire to set aside Western culture's expressions of faith and "help the African make it his very own" or to "translate Christianity into the idiom of the African's soul." Why? Because Crocker believed whatever aesthetic form it took, Christianity offered in terms of morality something the African "is unable really to assimilate and which therefore will lead to a simulating of something he has not got and so to a moral poison."[13] He further claims that "of the several million professing converts in Nigeria there can be but a handful who have really arrived at an elementary understanding of Christianity, and whose lives are genuinely and deeply affected by it."[14] For "it is," he says, "too much to ask [of] an animist African."[15]

In similar fashion Edmund Morel, who was not an administrator but rather a rubber merchant in Lagos and member of the West African Section of the Liverpool Chamber of Commerce, who was in favor of maximum British commerce and minimum political interference, and who had zero tolerance for Christian missionary "meddlesomeness," suggested with regard to West Africa that "Islam might prove to be intended as the half-way house through the portals of which it was necessary the... negro should pass in order to lift him out of a sterilizing paganism and make him a fitter vessel to receive in course of time the nobler ideas of the Christian faith."[16]

And yet many pagans skipped over Islam and became Christians. Thus Crocker writes that "nothing very much can be done" about Nigerians converting to Christianity. Why? Because—so Crocker claims—the African believes "the white man's juju" is superior to his own; Christianity "supplies free, or very cheap, reading and writing lessons"; and the hymns and services "appeal to his love of community singing and ritual."[17]

Likewise Lugard blamed conversions to Christianity on the black man's love of music and showing off. He writes, "Christianity... has a most powerful auxiliary in its hymns and church music, which are infinitely attractive to him, as well as the frequent occasions it affords for a display of oratory."[18]

Lugard writes further that "it has sometimes been alleged that the Governments of the Sudan and Nigeria favour Mohamedanism. The attitude which the British Governments have endeavoured to assume is that of strict neutrality, impartiality, and tolerance in all religious matters."[19]

This simply is not true. Lugard and other British administrators in Northern Nigeria strongly favored Islam. They did so on the basis of Darwinian racism.

Figure 6.1. Missionary Walter Miller with two Hausa students from Northern Nigeria in 1925.

6. Anti-Darwinian Christians

BECAUSE THEY INSISTED UPON ELEVATING THE LIGHT-SKINNED Islamic Fulani, British authorities in Northern Nigeria found themselves in a difficult position: they were promoting Islam while, at the same time, they needed to allow Christian missionaries because "such activity was essential to legitimizing colonialism to the home audience."[1]

Thus British administrators in Northern Nigeria allowed some missionaries, yet threw up obstacles designed to make the endeavors of those missionaries unsuccessful. Other missionaries they blocked entirely, as we shall see, justifying this with the claim that they feared conflicts between Christians and Muslims, although "in the areas where Christian missions operated [in the north] there was not a single instance of Muslims rising against Christian adherents."[2]

Moreover, missionaries were willing and available to cooperate with government officials on development projects for the common good.[3] The problem was not the missionaries, but the administrators. After working in missionary service for almost forty consecutive years in Northern Nigeria, Walter Miller wrote:

> The many restrictions put upon our work were deemed necessary by a Government which was ruling a huge African protectorate with a very small number of white men. I could see neither the necessity nor the wisdom of this plan [of restrictions]; and felt that a bolder policy would have been equally safe or safer, and in the long run have made for the truer blessing of the country... It was always a great burden to me to see

work that might have been done so easily, and with such good results, prohibited.[4]

Bureaucracy by its nature restricts. But in truth, the primary problem was that British administrators and Christian missionaries had widely different views of Nigerians. Missionaries had a higher view of local peoples and "held a perspective on African culture that was contrary to that of indirect rule."[5] For this reason, English missionaries were the fiercest critics of British misrule in Northern Nigeria, and often reported problems administrators would have preferred to keep quiet. It is telling that Lugard declined to allow the missionary Miller's book to be dedicated to him, and also refused to write the foreword.[6] Two other British administrators, Lieutenant Governors E. Arnett and H. Goldsmith, wrote rebuttals of Miller's descriptions of certain incidents in his book.[7]

Mr. Morgan, a former Resident of Kabba Province, further identifies a problem which has not been admitted publicly by any other government functionary: jealousy of the missionaries by government functionaries. He writes:

> The [missionary] mixes among them in a much more intimate way than the European Official has time to do, and very often treats them more as human beings, and less as mere Black men.
>
> Sometimes a Missionary gets a wonderful hold over the native people of his district. He is their "guide, philosopher and friend." They take all their palavers to him to settle, and some-times the European official is jealous of the Missionary. Why should he be? The Missionary is perhaps on the spot, whereas the European Official is distant a couple of days' journey. The Official should be glad of the Missionary's co-operation, and welcome it. What does it matter which of them settles a palaver as long as it is settled, and the people are kept quiet and peaceable?[8]

Christian missionaries knew the people among whom they labored far better than did the administrators. As Miller wrote, "We lived among the people, and were easily accessible by day or night."[9] By contrast, "The usually hard-worked Divisional officer, or his Assistant Divisional officer, rarely stays long enough in a village to realize the conditions of village life. I have spent weeks in these villages, living with the people, heard their stories... and spent hours at night telling them stories and listening to theirs."[10]

Thomas Bowen, the first Southern Baptist missionary in Yorubaland, pushed back against the Social Darwinist notion that Nigerians were inferior races morally. He wrote that in the Yoruba character there was "much to admire and much to condemn," as is the case with all people.[11] As he wrote:

> I am not sure that the Negroes are more covetous than other people, though they are less careful to hide the love of dishonest gain. If they swindle and lie, there are thousands in our own country who are guilty of the same practices. If fair dealing is one of the last things learned by the converts in the missions, honesty, both in everyday life, and in religious controversies, is one of the rarer virtues among too many members and teachers in the churches of civilized countries. It has not been many years since a noble bishop declared that "he knew nothing of moral obligation," in the use of certain revenues of the church. Custom was his authority for transactions which appeared to some members of Parliament and many Englishmen like swindling, and custom is the plea for the African when he cheats you in buying and selling. He will not steal but he will defraud to the utmost of his power.[12]

Bowen further asserts that "there are various... indications of the fact that the people are not deficient in intellect," and goes on to show that "one of these we find in the government and law":

> The highest excellence of the best governments among white people consists in constitutional checks or limits to prevent abuses of power. Strange as it may seem, the [Yoruba] had studied out this balance of power and reduced it to practice, long before our fathers settled in America—before the barons of England had extorted the great charter from King John. The pure and correct theism, which rises far above the superstitions of the people, is another proof of their mental soundness. Even their idolatry, while it is substantially the same as that of Assyria, Greece, and Rome, has not been loaded with such puerile fancies and debasing dogmas as were common at Corinth and Athens.[13]

Bowen, who lived among the people and learned to speak Yoruba fluently, stated categorically that "no one can live among the people and speak their language without being convinced that they have a good share of sober common sense. They are shrewd observers of character and motives."[14] He noted, further, that "very often there is both an abstract and a concrete noun for the same verbal root [in Yoruba language]. The existence and constant use of terms for the expression of thought, are certainly good evidence that the people think."[15]

He observed that the Yoruba deal much in proverbs, and that those of the Yoruba "are among the most remarkable proverbs in the world."[16] Their proverbs, he says, "are designed to convey moral truth. They constitute, in fact, the moral science of the nation, and being widely known and often quoted, have doubtless had a powerful effect in forming and preserving the character of the people."[17]

Thus missionaries had a higher view of Africans than did most British administrators.

Notice that Bowen referred to the Yoruba *language*. Colonial governments and their functionaries called European languages such as English, French, and German *languages*, but referred to African languages as *vernaculars*—something evolving en route to a language. On this point, Christian missions could not disagree more. To them, across the board, African tongues were languages. Thus Christians have developed numerous Nigerian orthographies and Bible translations, some of which are ongoing today.[18] No other religion or agency comes close to Christian missions in putting smiles on the faces of ethnics after ethnics for decades, as their languages are restored to a place of belonging, with all the benefits that follow.

Moreover, many missionaries showed a great appreciation for local culture. By 1900 one missionary with Nigerian experience was warning that missionary schools should not "endeavour to turn out black Englishmen."[19]

Clearly Christian missions do not go everywhere as instruments or forerunners of imperialism, but rather show a respect that neither colonists nor Islam shows. In point of fact, Christian missions restored the human dignity that the colonial administrators assaulted with their Social Darwinist ways.

That is not to say that Christians and Christian missionaries were without any faults. They resorted to Darwinist vocabulary from time to time when terms like "native" and "races" popped out of their mouths or appeared in their written literature, for they were children of their own generation. Nonetheless, it is equally true to point out that missionaries were not ideologically committed to such terms, which in fact contradicted rather than corresponded with their Bible-based view of the dignity of all humanity. Thus they kept updating and upgrading their knowledge of their host community and people generally, and so we see Ethel Thamer speaking of "great get-togethers for whites and nationals" and adding that "they are not to be called natives anymore."[20] Similarly, in Adamawa Province, Niels Høegh Brønnum, the pioneer Danish missionary in Nigeria, in 1913 was pleased to see terms such as "natives" replaced by "Africans" and "Nigerians" in missionary vocabulary.[21]

And then there is the matter of presentation. In order to excite pity and charity for Africans and maintain the flagging interest of European Christians in the missions abroad, missionaries tended to present the unconverted African in the worst possible light (showing the necessity of continuing missionary work) while also presenting Africans as most docile, most teachable persons (showing that the missionaries were succeeding). This dual purpose is discernible in practically every missionary publication, as distinct from the letters and some of the private journals. This is not to imply, however, that the publications were therefore deliberate distortions.

Benefits of Christian Missions

HISTORICALLY CHRISTIAN missions were attractive to Nigerians for a number of reasons, which shall here be briefly enumerated.

First and of great importance, Christians carried the spiritual good news of the worth and dignity of all peoples, believing as Christians do that all people, regardless of skin color or geographical location, are made in the image of God. This belief and the message of equality and of salvation through Christ did not originate in the West, of course; but in keeping with the Great Commission, Christians carried the good news worldwide.[22]

Christian missions also brought with them the "Bible and the Plough" ideology, that is, an emphasis on the harnessing of faith and diligence in the life of the Christian believer. The idea was not new in Africa, especially in primal religions. However, the affirmation was reassuring for the converts, that diligence has no substitute.[23]

Christian missions encouraged agriculture in the planting of cash crops and fruit trees, including the cultivation of cocoa,[24] coffee, and vines,[25] along with fruit trees such as mango, and also watermelons.[26] The Church of the Brethren Mission introduced new crops such as strawberries, and new species of cows to Adamawa Province in the late 1920s.[27] They trained in various skills and vocations such as architecture, town planning, road building;[28] brickmaking and brickworks, carpentry, and dyeing;[29] furniture making,[30] masonry,[31] clock repair,[32] tilemaking,[33] shoemaking, tailoring, iron work, cookery, and gardening,[34] among others.

Christian missionaries introduced new industries such as cotton gins and encouraged international trade in African goods. One of the earliest functions of the Church Mission Society (CMS) Industrial Institution at Abeokuta, and later of similar institutions at Onitsha and Lokoja, was to encourage the cultivation and export of cotton by giving instruction in cleaning and packing cotton. For this reason, Henry Robinn and Josiah Crowther had been trained in Manchester. By 1861 there were already some three hundred gins at Abeokuta, a few at Ibadan and Ijaye, and some were beginning to ascend to the Niger. There were also a couple of grinding mills at Abeokuta, and in 1863, a European trader erected a steam-powered mill at Aro (near Abeokuta).[35]

Some Christian missions participated in international trade in African goods as of the 1870s. This was their response to the stark monopoly

Figure 6.2. Bishop Samuel Ajayi Crowther, the first African Anglican bishop in Nigeria, opposed the monopolistic practices of the United African Company.

of European trading companies, whom they accused of taking away resources and bringing to Africans trifles and toys on the one hand and gin and rum on the other. To this end, some of the missions set up trade rules to ensure that their converts got value for their produce. In contrast, some of the trading companies, for example in Yola Province, still engaged in trade by barter and encouraged unfair practices, whenever the administrators looked the other way, throughout the period Charles Temple was Lieutenant Governor of Northern Nigeria.

Bishop Samuel Ajayi Crowther, the first African Anglican bishop in Nigeria, was an example of opposition to the monopolistic practices of the United African Company (later the Royal Niger Company). Since he was a shareholder in the West African Trading Company, courtesy of Henry Venn, who bought some shares for him, he defied the takeover of all the smaller British companies, as well as the French and German interests east of the Niger. For example, he got a disused ship refurbished which went north and south of the Niger and Benue. His second son later became the Agent-General of the company, thereby aggravating an already ignition-ready hatred by the Royal Niger Company.

In more recent years, rather than respond with relief materials which act as nothing but a palliative for a season, the Church of the Brethren Mission in the northeast of Nigeria launched a loan plan to transform the economy of the farmers in their local communities—not just their converts—into owners of better means of production beyond one season. In some cases, for life. According to a testimony of the times,

> An agricultural program of the Church of the Brethren Mission in Nigeria in 1957 established a loan program to enable farmers to buy teams of oxen and plows. Poor farmers who previously had used the hand hoe were thereby able to raise their standard of living by increasing their production of food. These farmers were then able to pay fees for the education of their children and were in a better position to support the work of the church both with time and financial contributions.[36]

In addition to economic advances, Christian missionaries brought an interest in journalism, printing, and publishing. For example, the Presbyterians arrived with a printer and a printing press, and they began publication on the spot almost at once. In August 1849, the printer listed that he had produced 800 copies of the Primer, 500 copies of Bible lessons, 150 of Arithmetical Examples, 200 of multiplication tables, 500 almanacs with the Commandments in Efik, 300 copies of *Elementary Arithmetic*, and 400 of the Catechism in Efik and English. By publishing on the spot, the printer was training some apprentices.[37]

Having published pamphlets, hymns, catechism, and prayers, and undertaken some binding for some time, Henry Townsend of the CMS took the publishing industry to a new level in 1859 when he "began to publish the *Iwe-Irohin*, a fortnightly journal in Yoruba giving news of Church and state from near and far, and educating the growing reading public through didactic essays on history and politics. In the following year an English supplement was begun, and a missionary observed that one new feature of the civilised world was introduced, an advertisement column declaring vacancies for apprentices, clerks, houseboys, and others."[38]

Further:

Townsend's example was soon followed. Robert Campbell returned to Lagos in 1862 and almost at once founded the *Anglo-African*. His printers came from the C.M.S. printers in Abeokuta. In that way, Townsend had contributed to the keen interest in journalism and the technical excellence of many of the newspapers that began to appear in Lagos in the succeeding years. It may also be claimed that the large number of one-room printing works in several large towns in Nigeria owes something to the same source.[39]

Christian missionaries introduced various medical services. They took a keen interest in medical services because there is no way of making a radical distinction between the care for the soul and the body in Christian witness. Admittedly, there are situations and contexts when one of the two may be prioritized; however, ultimately, they are bound together. It is, therefore, not surprising that Samuel Crowther, Jr., the eldest son of Bishop Crowther, who studied medicine in London, had established a dispensary in Abeokuta by 1852,[40] in lieu of a full-fledged hospital. Thomas Bowen, whose earlier training was not medical, took a diploma course to participate in medical care while at Calabar, and the Presbyterian missionaries did all within their power to vaccinate against smallpox.[41]

Finally, the impact of mission-based Western education, which arguably should be the first, is reserved for the last to equally make the point that education is so important that none of the other items or services of impact could have been possible without the underlying impact of Western education introduced by the missions. In fact, by the time Northern Nigeria Protectorate was proclaimed, products of Western education in the Lower Niger had been practicing law, medicine, teaching, and many of the professions which let them stand on their feet in a changing world. One only needs to consult the lecture delivered by Governor William MacGregor of Lagos in London, 1904.

And we could go on and on. The areas of Nigeria that saw plentiful and unrestricted Christian missions benefitted greatly from their presence. Christian missionaries saw the African to be as capable of comprehending and embracing Christianity as any European, and as capable of learning and implementing advances in any number of other fields as well.

Thus it is eminently reasonable for the missionary Miller, who found himself thwarted so often in Northern Nigeria, to ask the following question:

> The typical missionary is a man whose best years are spent in seeking to assimilate the customs, language, and manners of the people among whom he lives. Can it be honestly contended that in a Mohammedan land, where railways are being laid down, trade is coming in from all quarters, and prospecting for minerals and large mining operations are being undertaken, which involve the presence of engineers, foremen, labourers, traders, and prospectors, all of whom are seeking a living and many of whom are only out for a year, and who are utterly out of touch with all that concerns the chief things of the life of the people—can it be contended that the missionary is the one harmful disturbing element, that he alone is to be kept out?[42]

Obstacles to Christian Missions in Northern Nigeria

The multitude of benefits described above were some of the realities of which the emirs in the southern regions of the Upper Niger could not remain ignorant. They did not need to be told that they were going around in a circle as far as development was concerned. And the emirs were determined to do something about it.

Professor Emmanuel Ayandele states that for eighteen years (1870–1888), emirs wrote letters asking Christian missionaries to come to their domains to begin missionary enterprise. His upper limit of 1888 is because he did not account for the letter written by the emir of Keffi, 1896, for a missionary presence in Keffi.[43] That is correct: the Muslim emirs at the southern fringes of the Upper Niger wrote letters inviting Christian missionaries to come and establish missions in their domains.

So here we have Muslims requesting Christian missionaries—not for spiritual gain, it is true, but because they recognized that Christians had brought with them elsewhere in Africa a wide range of positives. Muslim rulers themselves, by virtue of their letters to European missions, provided the fuel, data, evidence, and exhibits for Europeans to believe that Christianity was a better alternative for Africa than Islam.

British administrators such as Lugard, however, persistently discouraged Christian missionaries in Northern Nigeria, throwing various obstacles in their way. Islam they had chosen, and Islam they wished to retain.

One confusion which must be cleared up: Walter Miller, the first CMS medical missionary to the Hausa people in Northern Nigeria, erroneously portrayed Lugard as "a great Christian."[44] Miller thought this because Lugard allowed him to open the Hausa CMS Station in 1904, following the failed attempt in 1900. Other observers saw Lugard differently. Margery Perham, Lugard's friend and biographer, described him as a man of little religion who "lost his old faith" and "groped for some system by which to explain his own morality" to which he added "the pride of the agnostic."[45] Likewise Sonia Graham, who studied Lugard's treatment of Christian missionary efforts, identified him as an agnostic.[46]

Other British administrators opposed Christian work in Northern Nigeria as well. Temple concedes, "The Government of Northern Nigeria, with which I was long privileged to be connected, has, I fear, earned a rather bad reputation amongst the religious bodies because in respect to a large portion of those territories the establishment of missions was not only not encouraged but prohibited."[47] Temple then explains that in his view, missionaries introduce too quickly "ideas conceived by other more civilised races," to the detriment of the native, who leaps "from feudal to modern social conditions in the course of a few short years."[48]

Ayandele notes that "evidence is plentiful to show that after 1906 the administration of Northern Nigeria became decidedly anti-missionary."[49] He explains:

> A missionary was likely to be a rival to the Resident's influence and, as a man close to the poorer classes, was likely to be the tribune of the oppressed. The British missionaries in those years were more than religious teachers; they saw themselves as watchdogs of Britain's interest and they never hesitated to bring to the notice of either the Colonial Office, or the public, acts of oppression and injustice committed by administrative officers in Nigeria.[50]

Further, Ayandele notes, "by 1905 some of the Residents had begun to deplore the doctrine of equality of all peoples—white and black—before God, which they alleged the missionaries were teaching."

Thus increasingly throughout the years, administrators in Northern Nigeria sought ways in which to stymie mission work. Notable actions include, in 1915, the establishment of the segregational "440-yard rule" prohibiting European residences from being located within a quarter mile of a Nigerian community—a rule that "had its origin with Lugard himself."[51] The rule as enacted was bad, but it was better than the initial proposal of a one-mile segregation. About that Charles Temple writes:

> A European trader, or especially a European barrister, planted in the middle of a big native town might have a more disintegrating effect than a mission station. But the Government can control and educate its own officials, and it can segregate the white community, but it cannot educate or segregate the missionary. Though I advocate strongly the segregation of Europeans from the bulk, at all events, of the natives in tropical Africa, yet in the case of the missionary I hold that to do so is altogether illogical and unreasonable. Setting aside the political officers, whose position resembles that of the missionaries, all other Europeans can carry out their duties without living in close contact with natives; but a missionary cannot. If he is to live a mile away from any native hut he might as well go home altogether. He must, to do his work at all, live his life among the natives.
>
> In such circumstances I think it may be admitted that among certain sections of African natives in certain stages of development it may

behoove the Government to consider the feasibility of permitting the establishment of mission stations.[52]

Thus even Temple, who disliked missionaries and whose general slogan was expressed as "just keep the missionaries and the lawyers out!" saw separating missionary homes from the locals by a full mile as "illogical and unreasonable."

True to form, Temple did, however, go on to argue against admitting Christian missionaries on the grounds that the feelings of the "Muhammadan communities" and "pagan tribes" must be taken into account, along with the risk of political discord. If missionaries there must be, he argued, let them go to pagan areas, for "the primitive instinct is strong within him and makes him cling to his tribe, to his environment, to his hereditary customs." Unlike the supposedly more-advanced Muslim, the pagan faces "little or no danger of losing his characteristics readily or of his trying to ape the white man."[53]

The missionary J. L. Maxwell objected vociferously to any separation, saying the law forced a missionary "to do the big thing and get away from the people and sit alone, alone with a vengeance, instead of coming quietly in among a people living among them continually till they know you and trust you and listen to what you have to say."[54]

Nevertheless, the segregationist quarter-mile rule was sanctioned, ostensibly for the protection of missionaries from yellow fever and other nameless bugs. These bugs apparently could discriminate between the blood of missionaries and the blood of the hosts; and could recognize the boundary of Northern and Southern Nigeria—and the bug was unknown in Southern Nigeria! Many missions were forced to relocate, with unplanned expenses.[55]

In 1930 the colonial government introduced the eighteen-year rule, ostensibly to protect Muslim female minors under eighteen years of age from contact with even missionary females to forestall the probability of coercion or pressure from Christian missionaries on Muslim minors to convert to Christianity. In this, as in so many other decisions by British Administrators, Islam was privileged while Christianity lost out.

Years earlier, in 1912, Miller—who as we shall see behaved with great tact and delicacy regarding Islamic religious beliefs—had questioned this policy of strenuously protecting Muslims from encountering Christian ideas. He writes:

> Now it must be remembered that wherever a Moslem goes he is a missionary! Why, then, does a Christian Government enforce the *Pax Britannica* and compel these pagan peoples to permit Mohammedan traders and malams (teachers) *all practising and teaching their religion* to come and live and trade among them, teaching their children and perverting them against their will, and, as we know, to their disgust and sorrow, for at present the hatred of Islam is deep and bitter?

> …. The Moslem trader and teacher may go among the Christianised peoples further afield, and, getting among those who are only half-trained and are not truly Christian, may find fields for conquest. But when Christian missionaries claim the same privilege to go to the Moslem, he is liable to be told that they have their faith, that he must not disturb them, and that Government is pledged not to interfere with their faith! Does anyone wish to *interfere* with their faith?

> …. If Government is not prepared to let Christian missionaries settle in Mohammedan countries, then why not plainly say to Mohammedan Emirs, "If you wish and claim that Christians should not come to your lands and speak to your people about their faith, then you must stop all your people from going into Christian and pagan countries, either for trade or teaching." I merely write thus to show to what *reductio ad absurdum* we are reduced if we attempt to follow out fairly and logically to its rational conclusion such an interpretation of the policy of Neutrality! Why should Moslem communities under Christian Governments be treated as close preserves?[56]

Historically, Christianity undeniably has sometimes been commandeered for non-Christian ends; however, in Northern Nigeria, perhaps because it was already daybreak in most places on earth, the British could not do the magic of commandeering Christianity. Thus the colonizers elevated Islam and feared Christianity and Christian missions. Why? Because Christianity and Social Darwinism are inherently and diametrically opposed.

Figure 7.1. Book by Charles Lindsay Temple, who opposed "the extension of the system of European education to the great majority of [Nigerian] natives who are still untouched."

7. EDUCATION: KEEPING THE DARK MAN IN THE DARK

AN OPPOSITION BY BRITISH COLONIAL RULERS TO CHRISTIAN MIS-
sions in Northern Nigeria meant a congruent opposition to education.

C. N. Adiche writes that "in the North, missionaries and their
Western education were discouraged, to prevent what Frederick Lugard
called their 'corrupting influence' on Islamic schools."[1] Ayandele agrees
that "in Northern Nigeria the missions were not allowed to do institu-
tional work. The school for Emirs' children and malams proposed by
the CMS in 1906 foundered on the opposition of the Residents. Not
a penny was given to Christian missions for the very little educational
work they embarked on."[2]

However, Ayandele further points out that "even the traditional Koranic schools received no encouragement."[3] What are we to make of this?
The British administrators preferred, it seems, to keep the Dark Continent entirely in the dark.

Thus while in Eastern Sudan mission-educated Africans were by
1915 holding posts in the administration, in 1920 Northern Nigeria,
there was as yet not one Northern Nigerian with sufficient education
to fill even a low-level government post.[4] This no doubt was fine with
Lugard, who wrote in a memorandum that "it is so hard to find honest
Native subordinates" and who urged his Residents to take a general position of mistrust toward Nigerians.[5]

Charles Temple sought to discount Northern Nigeria's educational failures by arguing that education along European lines does not benefit the "native" but rather separates him from his own people. Thus he claims that it is *good* that Northern Nigeria produced no such educated men, for reading and writing English violates the "natural order."[6] Indeed, Temple advocated "bringing back these natives into the fold of normal native evolution."

He said, "I hotly oppose the extension of the system of European education to the great majority of natives who are still untouched, who I hold can, without dislocation or damage to anybody, be encouraged and assisted to develop on lines natural to them to become valuable members of the Empire."[7]

Thus, holding firmly to Social Darwinist principles regarding the "lower races," Temple argued against educational practices that would enable the Nigerian to participate in global affairs, in which English is the language of trade and communication. (Even by 1900 English was the language of globalization.)

The missionary Walter Miller recorded in his autobiography that he urged Lugard and his administrators to make English instruction available:

> Our talk after dinner turned upon what might seem to many a very trivial matter, but which to me was vital. It was this: Should we retain the Arabic script already in use throughout the whole of the Northern Provinces, the script for Moslem literature, the Kur'an and the Traditions, or the Roman character which would one day make the youth of Northern Nigeria heirs of the literature of Greece and Rome and Judaea and the whole civilized world. Among the senior men, administrators whom Lugard had brought with him, the almost unanimous verdict was for Arabic.[8]

Lugard himself did not rule out the teaching of English, reasoning that by learning English the African could prove himself useful to the British authorities[9]; but he never put in place any effective means of instruction. To his mind English could be taught, but Arabic took precedence because it was the language held dear by Muslims. Thus Lugard expressed contradictory views. He wrote, "No greater benefit can be conferred on the African, whether as a means of enabling him to make known his desires, or for purposes of trade, or as affording an access to a great literature, than the teaching of English as a universe medium."[10] Yet he also wrote: "The goal of their ambition is to read the Koran, and to study the laws and traditions of Islam. No Mohamedan considers that he can claim to be properly educated unless he is able to do this. His outlook is towards the literature of the East—not of the West."[11] Lugard had no real intention other than getting the sons of emirs educated—in Arabic[12]—and his intentions did not change even when it became clear that, as he himself conceded, "in Sokotu and Bornu, the religious headquarters in East and West—English is becoming more popular than Arabic."[13]

Further, it was later decreed that "only children who had attended lessons in reading and writing in the local vernacular might attend English instruction."[14] The "local vernacular" meant Hausa. Some spoke Hausa as their second language, but many did not. Thus it came to pass that Northern Nigerians who spoke other African languages could not be taught English until they learned Hausa first!

While it is respectful to treat Nigerian languages as legitimate, what point was there in taking Nigerians who spoke their own various languages and erecting before them the barricade of a different Nigerian tongue, prior to allowing them to learn the international tongue of English? Why impose Arabic on all, or Hausa?

As Sonia Graham explains, the needs of Nigeria were not uniform. There was "the need for education for Moslems on the one hand, and on the other for the non-Moslems of many tribes, speaking different languages, and not using Hausa as a *lingua franca*." However, "Since the Moslem character of the Hausa states was being supported by the Administration, the education of Moslems was the most pressing question and the one that would show the quickest practical benefits from the

Government's point of view. The education of Moslems would be a better immediate investment."[15]

But this was a problem, for Christian missions were the primary source of education. If Christians were considered unsuitable educators for Muslims, whose education took precedence over that of non-Muslims, then the education of all became hindered.

Miller attempted to work with Lugard to bridge this gap, promising that he would "not interfere with his pupils' religious observances nor use his position to force anything upon them." He did, however, quite reasonably reserve the right to speak of Christian tenets.[16] However, bureaucratic tangles and conflicting goals amongst governmental committees back in Britain—some of whom favored strictly secular schools and some of whom favored teaching all students Christianity during school hours—along with the aforementioned opposition from Residents—resulted in the eventual failure of Miller's attempt.[17]

Although Lugard had agreed to work with Miller, he preferred secular schools and was no doubt relieved. As an agnostic, Lugard wished to teach morality "unsanctioned by religion," whereas the missionaries argued that "moral instruction without a systematic and definite religious basis is not of sufficient force to overcome the natural proclivities."[18]

Graham writes that according to Miller, "Lugard freely admitted that he disliked the idea of Christian missionaries working among the Moslems, but 'he quite understood that he had no reason for keeping us out of any part of this country except where there were definite troubles anticipated.'"[19] From this point on, Graham says, "mission societies were to find it increasingly difficult to extend their spheres within Northern Nigeria, and the CMS's hope of developing mission education throughout the Moslem provinces was not only dead, but damned."[20]

In 1908, Governor Percy Girouard, the man who replaced Lugard and who would also be replaced by Lugard, commissioned Hans Vischer, a Swiss CMS missionary[21] turned British citizen and thereafter a colonial officer, to study the education systems of Egypt, Sudan, Gold

Coast, and Southern Nigeria with a view to recommending a suitable system for Northern Nigeria.

Unfortunately, after the junketing to distant places, Vischer recommended and got approved the Sudanese model, with Arabic as its lowest common denominator. The "extension of government schools to non-Moslem areas was to be considered after the successful establishment of Moslem schools," while (unfunded) mission schools would be allowed to instruct non-Moslems, contingent upon inspection by the Education Department. Pursuant to acceptable inspection, mission schools might be awarded grants.[22] But in a situation where most of the Residents wished to do away with Christian missions, where were the objective assessors of Christian mission schools? And what chance had those schools of securing grants?

Thus, again, education for Muslims took precedence over education for non-Muslims.

Further making the bias against non-Muslim education apparent, in 1916 Article 13e was inserted into the Education Ordinance: "No grant shall be made to any school or training institution which is a Mission or other Christian school or training institution situated in a District of the Northern Province in which no mission or other Christian school or training institution is established at the commencement of the Ordinance."[23] In other words, mission schools could not receive funding if they wished to go into areas that did not already have schools.

The CMS bishop in Lagos mobilized public opinion in Southern Nigeria and in Britain against this obnoxious anti-missions insertion by the Colonial Office, and the detestable provision was expunged in July 1917. But "the government published in August 1917 new regulations which tightened the government's control over mission schools in Northern Nigeria."[24] Graham notes, "Clause 13e was withdrawn only to be replaced by the further Ordinances in 1918 and 1919 which provided even greater control over mission schools anywhere in the Northern Provinces.... The direct effect of the educational legislation of 1916 to 1918 was to prevent the extension of mission education without Government permission. Lugard had worked steadily towards this position of control, a position which he felt was justified by the example of uncontrolled educational expansion in Southern Nigeria."[25]

What dreadful things occurred by way of "uncontrolled educational expansion" in Southern Nigeria? Albert Ogunsola writes:

> In the Northern provinces there were only 954 children in school in 1912 as compared with 35,716 in the South. By 1926 the children in the Northern schools increased to 5,210 as compared with 138,248 in the South. The increase of over 400 percent for the Northern provinces was definitely phenomenal.... But when one considers that the North was almost 1½ the South in population it could not be anything but grim that the gap between the North and the South should be that wide—5,210 to 138,248.[26]

Southern Nigeria thrived while Northern Nigeria floundered, thanks to the Northern British administration's Social Darwinist policies.

In 1927 Alexander Fraser, principal of Achimota College, Gold Coast, was commissioned by Governor-General Graeme Thompson to appraise the education system of Northern Nigeria. Fraser began his study tour in Southern Nigeria (including Anglophone Cameroon), from March 21, 1927, to April 27, 1927. His tour of Northern Nigeria ran from April 27, 1927, to May 17, 1927. The ensuing forty-seven page report contained sixteen pages on Southern Nigeria, twenty-four pages on Northern Nigeria, and seven pages of appendix. The section on Northern Nigeria was sub-divided into two with seventeen pages dedicated to Northern Nigeria generally and seven pages dedicated to the "The Work among Pagans."

Fraser concluded that pagans had been "practically ignored" educationally[27] and, further, that in Northern Nigeria the cost of training a child was ten times more expensive than the cost of training a child in Southern Nigeria. He lamented that the "total number of children being educated in Northern Nigeria after twenty-five years of British rule was under 5,000." Most of those educated were the sons of emirs.[28]

Why was the cost of educating the princes in Northern Nigeria so high? It is not unreasonable to hypothesize that, first, it was not an accident, and secondly, that the amount allocated to the education of the princes was purposely to make education out of reach of the masses.

Fraser furthermore noted:

The best school I saw in the North, far and away the most efficient, was Miller's. The boys and girls in it, for he has both, were more intelligent and had a better appreciation not only of the sort of things that may be learned in schools, but of their own town and country, than any others I saw elsewhere. But then the teaching methods were not Koranic but were up-to-date; and the aim was to draw out intelligence everywhere and to develop it.[29]

That is, the best school he saw was a Christian mission school; and this school educated girls as well as boys. According to Fraser, "an amazing part of the Northern Programmes is that there are no girls in government schools, and at present there is no intention of catering for them. The Director said that this might be left to missions. But missions are not allowed into many areas and are rarely encouraged anywhere."[30]

Fraser concluded that Vischer and others, with their privileging of Islam and their anti-missionary stance, caused deplorable harm to Northern Nigeria. He observed,

Missionary education in the North hardly exists. It is only equal in extent to the Administration effort. Elsewhere missionary education is usually in the ratio to that of Government of at least four to one. But not so in the North. The reason for this is to be found in the continuing discouragement shown towards it by the Administration.... Missions might have freely been welcomed into Pagan areas, but they have been only grudgingly admitted.[31]

Fraser was convinced that Northern Nigeria was not fated for backwardness, but that the British administrators were architects of its disgraceful educational condition.

J. H. Oldham[32] promptly came to the defense of Vischer in a letter dated July 4, 1927, assuring Fraser, "No matter what you may have heard out there, I do not believe that Vischer was personally responsible to any large extent for the anti-missionary policy. He probably got his instructions from his superiors… Gowers, Temple and Palmer are an-other bunch altogether."

Be that as it may, Vischer was the Secretary of the Advisory Com-mittee on Native Education in British Tropical Africa that considered and then suppressed Fraser's report. But foreseeing the result—that his report would be suppressed from public view, as indeed it was—Fraser sent a copy to Governor Thompson, who had commissioned the study in the first place, and who was eager to carry out some reforms.

Years after Fraser submitted his report, and just thirteen years be-fore the end of colonial rule, Fraser wrote,

> I have seen a good deal of Administration work in Africa, chiefly in British and French Colonies. But considering its opportunities, I never saw anything more frozen, more static, than the condition of Northern Nigeria and the outlook of the Administration as a whole. I had the statistics of education before me, and I found that if the progress made under the first twenty-five years of British rule were to be steadily con-tinued at the same rate it would take 25,000 years to give education to every child in the North. If growth of the population was to be allowed for, it would take much more. The excuse was made that the Moslems did not desire education. But, I, a stranger, found a number who sent their sons to the Gold Coast to school, as there was not sufficient op-portunity for education close at hand. There was then, too, no attempt by the Administration to have girls educated.[33]

Governor Hugh Clifford, who took over from Lugard as Governor-General of Nigeria in 1919, noted regretfully:

> After two decades of British occupation, the Northern Provinces have not yet produced a single native… who is sufficiently educated to en-able him to fill the most minor clerical post in any office of any gov-ernment department…. The African staff of these offices throughout the Northern Provinces are therefore manned by men from the Gold Coast, Sierra Leone, and from the Southern Provinces in Nigeria…. Education in the North has been practically confined to the vernacular and to Arabic, has been allowed to become the exclusive prerequisites of the children of the local ruling classes, and has for its main object the

equipment of these children with just sufficient knowledge of reading, writing and arithmetic to enable them in after life to fill posts in one or another of the various Native Administrations.[34]

The retardation of education in Northern Nigeria and the widening gap between Northern Nigeria and Southern Nigeria was not fated. As Miller lamented, "All this might have been foreseen and prevented... many years ago, I pleaded for instruction in English, not only as a subject, but as the vehicle of instructions, realizing that English must certainly become the language both of literature and of commerce of the near future. It was in vain."[35]

In similar fashion Miller elsewhere lamented, "Vehement protests against educating the African at all, which one heard so frequently in the early days of the occupation of Northern Nigeria, have given way to a protest against the kind of education given. Negative again, and only a variant of the old die-hard fear of giving the African any 'place in the sun.'"[36]

Thus against the protests and efforts of Christian missionaries, Lugard educationally elevated the sons of Muslims while limiting non-Muslims to permanently playing second fiddle, and made Northern Nigerians inferior educationally to other Nigerians. Social Darwinist policies and perspectives kept the people of Northern Nigeria down and aided their so-called benefactors in achieving maximal exploitation and dehumanization.

Further Elevation of Islam

NOR WERE the harms of Social Darwinist attitudes and policies restricted only to education. In Northern Nigeria the light-skinned Islamic fared better than the dark-skinned pagan or Christian in a host of ways.

Consider that forced circumcision by a Muslim cleric was imposed on new pagan recruits to the army.[37] To place a mark on the private part of unsuspecting and powerless recruits was as strategic as it could possibly be. First, it lent to the pagan the notion that the army was a Muslim institution and that he was expected to convert, at least in public, to Islam. Secondly, the future offspring following the circumcision presumably would also follow Islam. Thirdly, it demonstrates the probability that Islam is the gateway for promotion in the army, hence pressure to conform if he wishes to advance.

Next consider that while the British did truly discourage the taking of slaves, little pagan girls and boys who were saved from slavery were given into the care of Moslem emirs. Some of the boys ended up as eunuchs and most of course ended up Muslim. The girls were used swell up the harems, with the probability of remaining a pagan in the harem being zero.

Further consider that the British administrator Charles Temple took money from the public treasury to build a minaret for a call to prayer in Kano. Moreover, attendance at Muslim festivals by government officials was a common practice that conferred the approval or backing of the government.

And then there was taxation. Kanawa and Fulani district heads received higher rewards than other district heads. This blatant preferential treatment was enacted, for example, in Borguland, where "Muslim chiefs [were] to keep 70% [of the] revenue [collected], while pagan chiefs could only keep 30%."[38] Since the British taxed the pagans more heavily than the Muslims, many Hausa converted to Islam if only by name for the purpose of lower taxes and even outright tax evasion.

Moreover, the Northern Nigerian government moved the regional capital from Zungeru to a more centrally located Kaduna in 1921 and created the Northern Advisory Council of Chiefs whose membership was entirely Islamic, drawn from the surrogates and tentacles of the same loathsome old jihad empire—this in a colony whose population was majority pagan. It stands to reason that this arrangement was not an accident but a grand design to ensure that council recommendations were in favor of Islam, to the exclusion of all the rest, despite the fact that "the rest" were in majority.

All this to elevate light-skinned Muslims who supposedly were evolutionarily advanced, and who supposedly were popular rulers. And yet the British at the same time eventually deposed and banished every emir because they posed a threat of insecurity and instability! As early as 1902, Lugard admitted in his Annual Report that "it had been a source of regret to me that the inclusion of each new Province under administrative control had been accompanied by the deposition of the ruling Emir."[39] All the same, Islam and its supposedly superior proponents must be elevated, and the supposedly inferior pagans penalized.

Thus Walter Crocker, participant-observer of colonial rule in Northern Nigeria, remarked that colonial administration in Northern Nigeria became "an occult science" consumed by "undue preoccupation with Islam and the Emirates to the neglect of the Pagan peoples."[40]

Bright Spots

THERE WERE a few bright spots in this sea of Social Darwinist machinations. Notable is Resident Captain Ruxton, an administrator who converted to the Christian faith while on duty in Northern Nigeria in 1913. He demonstrated initiative and took risks with admirable dexterity within the law.

First, while other Residents were busy perfecting their bulwarks against mission work in their respective provinces, not only did Ruxton readily approve missionary work in whichever province he was placed in charge, he did not even wait for missionaries to apply for permission to open mission stations; rather, he as Resident invited any mission he assessed most suitable for the task to come and start work among the people he felt were in need of that particular mission.[41]

Ruxton was said to be the only Resident to resist the government policy of Islamification: "From all one hears, he is resisting the Government pro-Islam tactics as far as Muri Province is concerned; they want to put the Pagans everywhere under emirs but he will not agree to it in this Province.... Lugard's promise was often appealed to as the ground for such policies."[42]

Tellingly, in 1934 Ruxton "prayed for deliverance from this malady: 'From contempt for what we are pleased to call the inferior races—which is a sin against God and treason to ourselves—may we be delivered be-fore it is too late."[43]

Most administrators, however, ranked light-skinned Muslims high-er than their darker-skinned peers, and made administrative decisions accordingly.

HAUSA WOMAN TRADER

Figure 8.1. Frederick Lugard, the British Governor of Nigeria, regarded
native Nigerian traders and business people as undesirables.

8. DARWINIAN LEGACY

THE BRITISH COLONIAL LEGACY IN NORTHERN NIGERIA IS NOT ALL woes. It has to its credit the enforcement of *Pax Britannica*, suppression of the slave trade, introduction of modern banking and currency, and the introduction of decennia census. Railways were laid and roads constructed connecting those railways. Rail and road were integrated with the waterways where applicable. In this way, goods from Northern Nigeria were easily evacuated to the coast for shipment to Britain, just as goods from the coast were much more easily transported to Northern Nigeria. The British contributions in the transportation sector improved considerably the overall economy in Nigeria generally and in Northern Nigerian especially.[1]

However, the negatives far outweigh the positives. Frederick Lugard did not encourage infrastructure, as did his colleagues in Southern Nigeria. He was not interested in good schools, hospitals, and social services.

As far as trade, he was only interested in caste and status, with docile lower-caste peasantry producing raw materials for European manufacturers.[2] He felt "every Hausa trader was one toiler less in the fields"[3] and resented the Hausas' desire to trade which, in Lugard's own words, resulted in "an undue tendency to desert the paths of productive industry and go to and fro through the country carrying goods on their heads for the pleasure of making a profit by barter." Lugard continues, "The problem is, how can this class be taxed except by tolls."[4]

In point of fact, he predominantly wanted "to control, or even in some spheres to prohibit, the business enterprise of his nation"[5] and "was no enthusiastic friend of business interests in Nigeria."[6] He "showed no sign of grasping the idea of an administration devoting itself to creating favorable conditions for trade" and in particular disliked traders from coastal areas, saying, "the immigrant black trader is by no means a desirable person." Nor did Lugard trust European traders.[7]

The Europeans were allowed to dominate, however. Walter Miller lamented that in Northern Nigeria, Europeans squeezed out local businesses.[8] Various European countries struggled among themselves for control of African commerce, and in doing so frustrated any initiatives for Africans to compete with them; indeed they formed cartels to eliminate African participation even on the African's own soil, let alone in transatlantic trade.

Not only did the trading companies erect barriers against participation in the competition in trading activities, but the government erected barriers against indigenous ownership in the means of production.[9] As William Geary observes, "The Land Tenure of Northern Nigeria is unique as the summit of absolute Government control not only of minerals but of land in Northern Nigeria and of all dealings therein, not only between Natives and non-Natives but between Natives and Natives."[10] Geary writes:

> In 1909 a committee sat in England, Northern Nigeria Lands Committee, to decide the tenure of land in Nigeria, but no Native was a member of the committee, and no Native gave evidence before the committee, and with one exception all the committee and all the witnesses were officials. As the result of their Report there was passed in 1910 the Land and Native Rights Proclamation, repealed and re-enacted in 1916, which after certain inflated language in the preamble, put the whole land [a third of India] under the control of the Government, and in effect abolished private property, and not only as to non-Natives but as between Natives forbidding alienation without the consent of the Government. The Government took power to grant certificates of occupancy to non-Natives and Natives.[11]

Thus even Lugard's biographer and friend, Margery Perham, concedes that with regard to business enterprise, contemporary Africans can "justifiably criticize their colonialist predecessors."[12]

I. F. Nicolson notes, "Many of the endemic problems of Nigerian government seem now to flow directly from Lugard's own characteristic decisions," such as

> his choice of conquest rather than peaceful penetration, followed by the decision to keep the institution of Fulani rule, while replacing each ruler by a creature of his own; there was the decision to impose direct taxation; the decision to keep out of the North the influence of missionaries, lawyers, traders, and civil administrators from other territories; the decision not to establish a capital in a commercial centre; there was a whole series of decisions to avoid contact and co-operation with the South, and to concentrate all power in one pair of hands.[13]

Nicolson attributes Lugard's harmful decisions to the fact that he was primarily a militarist and not an administrator. He notes that despite painting himself as a pacifist, "in Lugard's last few months as High Commissioner and 'pacifier' there was more bloodshed, massacre, destruction, and loss of life than there had ever been in the course of British intervention in Nigeria."[14]

Certainly Lugard was a militarist and prone to solving problems with bloodshed. This does not, however, in any way rule out Darwinian influences. It cannot be denied that foundational to Lugard's villainy was his Social Darwinist perspective regarding the peoples of Nigeria. It is clear the colonial government of Northern Nigeria had Social Darwinism as its directive principle of governance, an ideology that has never hidden its opposition to the Christian faith, ethics, and values—including that of the dignity and equality of all humankind.

Following Lugard's Lead

LUGARD AND his colleagues caused harm to Nigeria that continues to this day, not only through the Social Darwinist policies they implemented, but also through Lugard's continuing influence.

The Lugards, as recognized experts publishing their views in such places as the *Encyclopedia Britannica*, managed via propaganda to cover up the harm they and their likeminded colleagues inflicted, broadcasting "their simple message—Lugard good, rest bad; North good, rest bad; North a success, South a failure."[15] Despite the tatters in which they left Northern Nigeria, their "use of current ideas of race, evolution, prestige, patriotism, civilization, and duty managed to cover the whole scene with a swirling mist which concealed what they wished to conceal."[16]

A result of the Lugards' propaganda was "Northern Nigeria attracting the attention of the consciously 'superior' classes... that helped repel and antagonize the rest, the traders and missionaries busy and influential in the South, who might have had much to contribute to economic and social development in the North also, had their presence been encouraged."[17]

Thus Lugard directly damaged Northern Nigeria, and furthermore influenced others to follow his own destructive path, for they were "gravely prejudiced by what Lugard had done and by what he and his wife continued tirelessly to do from their carefully contrived eminence as internationally recognized authorities on the administration of dependent territories."[18]

The ongoing negative legacies remain frustrating, for they were by no means inevitable, but arose from the Social Darwinist policies of those looking for a reason to plunder the so-called Dark Continent. Again, it must be said that these Social Darwinist policies were a reasonable interpretation and application of Darwin's theories to colonization. As Ashley Montagu writes:

> If it is true that the appeal to Darwinian theory for support of a social system based on ruthless competition and exploitation of colonial peoples represents a misinterpretation of evolutionary theory, the conclusion seems inescapable that Darwin himself was the first to make this misinterpretation. The few passages in which Darwin mentions altruism and cooperation... are crowded out by numerous statements that appear to stand in direct and unequivocal contradiction to them.[19]

Thanks to Lugard's Social Darwinist attitudes and policies, Northern Nigerian British authorities could exploit the country, and then wring their hands and proclaim to assessors, in effect, "we have done our part. These Africans cannot make progress. They are fated for backwardness."[20]

Current Day

THE QUESTION might fairly be asked, "Why have Nigerians not proven them wrong?" Why, once freed from British interference, did Northern Nigeria not root out all the ills planted in that earlier era?

Would that it were easy to undo the work of Darwin, Lugard, and their ilk. In addition to the difficulty of undoing decades of harmful economic policies, consider only three ongoing ramifications of British colonial rule and the ranking of humans on Darwin's evolutionary ladder.

First, jealous rivalry. Albert Ogunsola's analysis shows that the gap between Southern Nigeria and Northern Nigeria education has continuing consequences to this day. As Ogunsola puts it bluntly, "It was not only unfair to the Northerners who were made to look inferior educationally but went a long way to undermine the economy of the North and laid the foundation of mistrust, jealousy and unhealthy rivalry among the Northerners and Southerners."[21]

Second, Sharia law. A group of researchers published in February 2021 an article titled "Customary and Religious Laws are Impeding Progress Towards Women's Health in Nigeria," detailing uncomfortable statistics on which the politicians and short-sighted mis-leaders would like to place a lid. The authors use the phrase "customary and religious laws" as a term for what Nigerians readily and correctly identify as Sharia law. Areas under Sharia law have high levels of HIV, female genital cutting, maternal death, child marriages, and so forth. It is in Northern Nigeria—especially the northernmost states—where the preponderance of these problems reside.[22]

Third, violence. While the colonial regime cannot be blamed for all Muslim-Christian violence of the most recent three decades, "a policy of partiality to any unit breeds imbalance and dysfunction in the whole system, which if it is not checked does lead to violence in the sector and indeed in the wider society."[23] This system of partiality as we have seen was in full force under British imperialism. Today Nigeria has one of the highest rates of the killing of Christians because of their faith globally.[24]

In these three areas and in others, in Northern Nigeria "the leaders sowed wind; and the people harvested whirlwind."[25] Frederick Lugard and his cohorts are long dead, but the effects of their Social Darwinist policies live on.

Were it not for British interference, neither a discriminatory educational system nor a harmful and untrue religious system would have been codified in my country and in the hearts and minds of my people. Social Darwinism as a directive principle of governance in Northern Nigeria was an instrument of dehumanization.

Once dehumanization has been experienced, recovering one's humanity and the full freedom of human agency and creativity requires more than mere time. It requires careful thought and deliberate effort to root out such pernicious ideas, and it requires faith in the goodness and forgiveness of a merciful God who wipes away every tear and makes all things new. It is my hope that this book will encourage such thought and effort in all who read it, and that they will find the faith and strength to move beyond the tear-stained past toward the bright clear dawning of a better day.

PART TWO:
WAS DARWIN RIGHT?

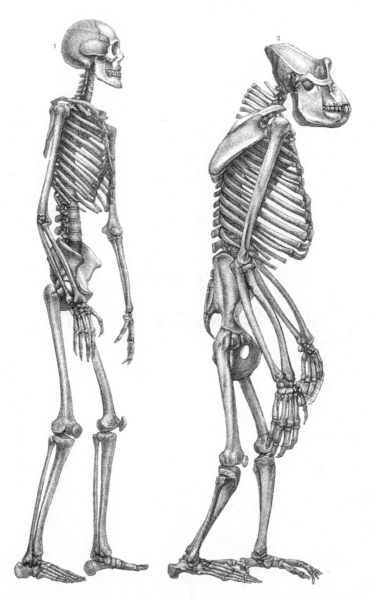

Figure 9.1. Comparison of human and gorilla skeletons, late nineteenth century.

9. Could Humans Have Evolved?

SOCIAL DARWINISM, THE IDEOLOGICAL SUPERSTRUCTURE ERECTED on Darwin's theory of evolution, deserves demolition because it obstructs and distorts the view of human beings as they really are, paving the way for the perpetuation of disinheritance, human rights violations, oppression, and dehumanization. But Social Darwinism cannot be thoroughly dismantled unless Darwin's theory itself fails, for if Darwin's theory is correct, then the structure built upon it has foundation. Here four questions will be posed, the answers to which demonstrate that Darwin's theory utterly fails.

The questions are these: Could humans have evolved in the way Darwin posits? Are humans nothing more than advanced animals? Are there differences that are both foundational and empirical between blacks and whites? Can human progress be categorized geographically, indicating that the people of certain regions are inferior or evolutionarily more primitive than those of other regions?

The answer to all is a resounding "NO!" We will take up the first question in this chapter, and the others in the subsequent three chapters.

To Build a Human

EVERY ORGAN in the human body is wonderfully crafted. Therefore, by highlighting two of them herein, I do not suggest that they are more important than the other organs of the human body. These are given merely as small examples typical of the whole.

The Eye

Charles Darwin himself set the ball rolling on the problem the human eye posed for his theory. Having beheld, calculated, pondered, and further reflected on the awesomeness of the human eye, and finding not enough words to express the irreducible complexity before his eyes, Charles Darwin found no alternative expression but to declare: "To suppose that the eye with all its inimitable contrivances for adjusting the focus to different distances, for admitting different amounts of light, and for the correction of spherical and chromatic aberration, could have been formed by natural selection, seems, I freely confess, absurd in the highest degree."[1]

Darwin in the next breath reversed himself as follows, saying

that *if* numerous gradations from a simple and imperfect eye to one complex and perfect can be shown to exist, each grade being useful to its possessor, as is certainly the case; *if* further, the eye ever varies and the variations be inherited, as is likewise certainly the case; and *if* such variations should be useful to any animal under changing conditions of life, *then* the difficulty of believing that a perfect and complex eye could be formed by natural selection, though insuperable by our imagination, should not be considered as subversive of the theory.[2]

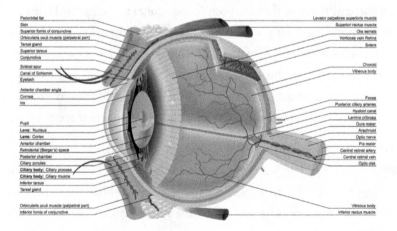

Figure 9.2. Anatomy of the human eye.

It is clear from the foregoing that Darwin's arguments for the evolution of the human eye are not based on fact but on three layers of "if."

Consider the interrelatedness and interdependence of the various parts of the human eye: the lens, the retina, the photoreceptors, the muscles, and the nerve for communications to the brain. Each of these involve myriad microscopic intricacies of its own. Biologists Michael Behe and Jonathan Wells have demonstrated "the irreducible complexity of the light-sensing cascade that makes vision possible,"[3] a feat far beyond the scope of unguided, directionless mutations even were some prehistoric light-sensitive spot a given, which it most certainly is not. Even supposedly simple eyespots have "high ultrastructural complexity."[4]

This is significant because gradual incremental change at each step along the way to a functioning eye would require all interrelated systems to make congruent changes, as physicist Brian Miller explains. He writes:

> The evolution of additional components in the vertebrate eye requires that this network of intercellular signals, TFs, TFBS, chromatin remodeling, as well as many other details be dramatically altered, so that each developmental stage can progress correctly. For instance, the seemingly simple addition of a marginally focusing lens—that is to say, a lens that directs slightly more light onto a retina—requires a host of alterations.... All of these steps must proceed with great precision... The challenge to evolution is that, short of completion, most of these changes are disadvantageous.[5]

To explain more clearly Miller uses an enlightening analogy: "In the context of fitness terrains, an organism lacking a lens resides near the top of a local peak. The steps required to gain a functional lens correspond to traveling downhill, crossing a vast canyon of visually impaired or blind intermediates, until eventually climbing back up a new peak corresponding to lens-enhanced vision."

Do not miss this point: The development of an eye lens requires a complex network of interacting genes to control the construction process. Hence, creating that genetic network would require hundreds if not thousands of highly specified genetic changes to occur at once for the lens to form properly; otherwise the tissue would block light from reaching the photoreceptors.[6] In other words, the evolutionist assemblage of thousands of mutations for a slight change to occur is a recipe for total blindness!

Furthermore, in a sequel to this article, Miller says:

Biologists have claimed to produce viable scenarios for the evolution of several other complex systems. What all these stories share is that they ignore crucial details and lack careful analysis of feasibility. When we examine these issues in detail, the stories collapse for the same reasons that the one about the eye does: First, the selective pressures oppose transitions between key proposed stages. Second, the required timescales [assigned by evolutionists] are vastly longer than what is available.[7]

Much more could be said about the eye and the impossibility of it evolving, unaided, in incremental steps.

The Ear

The ear likewise poses an insurmountable problem for Darwinian evolution.

The ear is roughly divided into three parts. The outer (external) ear includes the part you can see (called the pinna) and the narrow tube-like structure of the ear canal. The outer ear, or pinna, is shaped in such a way as to catch sound waves and direct the compressions and rarefactions of sound waves into the earhole, or auditory canal or meatus as some prefer to call it. The outer ear collects sound vibrations and directs them into the auditory canal.

The tympanic membrane, or eardrum in popular parlance, separates the outer ear from the middle ear. It is a layer of thin and yet tightly stretched circular tissue across the end of the canal, a bit like the skin of a drum. It has two functions: first, it separates the external ear from the middle ear. Second, pressure oscillations in the air from the outer ear are transferred via the tympanic membrane (eardrum) to three small bones in the middle ear (ossicles).

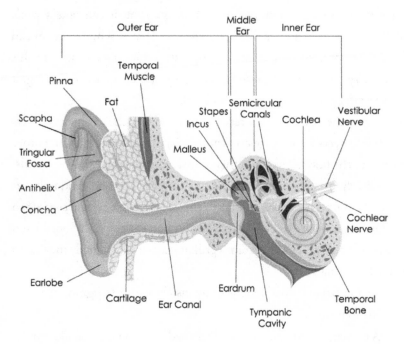

Figure 9.3. Anatomy of the human ear.

The middle ear is a small air-filled compartment between the eardrum and the inner ear. In the middle ear are the ossicles. These are the three smallest bones in the body, the malleus (hammer), incus (anvil), and stapes (stirrup), so called because of their shapes. These bones receive the sound waves from the eardrum and transmit them to the inner ear, while at the same time minimizing distracting background noises. The middle ear also contains the Eustachian tube, which connects the middle ear to the back of the nose. It helps equalize pressure, which is necessary for the proper transmitting of sound waves.

Finally comes the inner ear, consisting of the cochlea (a complicated chamber of bone shaped like a snail shell) and the vestibule, complete with a network of three looped tubes called the semi-circular canals. The vestibular system detects movement through special sensory cells which are activated as one's head tilts or moves. The system is ultra-sensitive to small movements of the head. (If one makes large, fast, or prolonged movements such as spinning around on the spot, it can take a while before the system settles down afterwards. That is why the room can appear to continue to spin when people stop spinning.) Thanks to this sensitivity, the vestibular system does not just play a part in hearing; it plays a vital part in maintenance of balance.

Once the sound waves reach the inner ear, the cochlea converts them into nerve impulses (electrical signals) that are sent by the auditory nerves to the brain. The brain then translates them into various sounds.

Clearly it is not simple for all this to gradually and randomly develop, each part in perfect sync with the others. Moreover, according to evolutionists we are to believe that the human ear thus developed from the reptile ear, supposedly from reptilian jaw bones gradually moving to form the human ear.

Again, Brian Miller's engineering insight assumes significance. According to him,

> A primary design constraint on therapsid [ancient mammal-like reptile] hearing is for the stapes to rigidly connect the sound receiver directly to the cochlea. In direct conflict, the corresponding design constraint on mammal hearing is for the stapes to connect to the incus. [Therefore] any mutation which disconnects the stapes in a therapsid would cause hearing to dramatically degrade. Hearing would not return to an operable level until the three bones needed for mammal hearing were perfectly reengineered to fit together, and they were properly connected through ligaments to each other and to the surrounding bone.

Furthermore, he insists, "natural selection would quickly remove the initial mutations preventing the transition from ever occurring."[8]

Since the human eye and the human ear could not evolve, what narrative option is open to evolutionists for the existence of the human body? Other organs and systems of the body contain myriad irreducible complexities of their own. The eye and ear are but two examples. And there are other obstacles to undirected evolution as well, such as the complementary binary of male and female in sexual reproduction, requiring the development of separate systems perfectly in sync with each other.

Evolutionists have no consensus regarding the path by which the human body came to be, positing many and various theories: Lamarck in 1809, neo-Darwinist theory, neo-Lamarckism (Jablonka), Gould and Eldredge's punctuated equilibrium, Kimura's neutral evolution, Lima de Faria's evolution without any selection, Schmidt's cybernetic evolution, McClintock's evolution by transposons, Goldschmidt's saltational evolution, and so forth.[9] As noted by Wolf-Ekkehard Lönnig, "None of these has ever produced a satisfactory explanation of the origin of species in general or of humans in particular."[10]

Consciousness

And the evolution of the body is not the only problem; materialist-based science has produced no evidence that consciousness could evolve into existence. Indeed, Dutch computer scientist and philosopher Bernardo Kastrup is adamant that consciousness could not have evolved, for "our phenomenal consciousness is eminently qualitative, not quantitative." He writes, "There is something it feels like to see the colour red, which is not captured by merely noting the frequency of red light." Such "felt qualities" are known to scientists as qualia, and

> qualities have no function under materialism, for quantitatively defined physical models are supposed to be causally-closed; that is, sufficient to explain every natural phenomenon. As such, it must make no difference to the survival fitness of an organism whether the data processing taking place in its brain is accompanied by experience or not: whatever the case, the processing will produce the same effects; the organism will behave in exactly the same way and stand exactly the same chance to survive and reproduce. Qualia are, at best, superfluous extras.

> Therefore, under materialist premises, phenomenal consciousness cannot have been favoured by natural selection. Indeed, *it shouldn't exist at all*; we should all be unconscious zombies, going about our business in exactly the same way we actually do, but without an accompanying inner life. If evolution is true... *our very sentience contradicts materialism* [emphasis in original].[11]

Darwinian evolution cannot account for the irreducibly complex body, nor can it account for consciousness.

MUSIC MAKERS OF BORNU, YOLA PROVINCE

Figure 10.1. Hausa musicians. Humans not only compose music—they create musical instruments to play their music.

10. ARE WE JUST ANIMALS?

To approach Darwinian and Social Darwinian claims from another angle, let us now consider the second question. Are humans nothing but advanced animals?

The chasm between animal and human is wide, and science has not bridged it. The ubiquitous image that shows an ape on the left and a human on the right, connected by a succession of figures gradually looking less ape-like and more human-like, is pure fiction. There is no evidence, in the fossil record or otherwise, that we gradually evolved from more primitive species. It is not there, nor will it be found. According to professor of anthropology Jeffrey H. Schwartz, "We should not expect to find a series of intermediate fossil forms with decreasingly divergent big toes and, at the same time, a decreasing number of apelike features and an increasing number of modern human features."[1]

Other leading paleoanthropologists agree. For one, Ian Tattersall cannot be more emphatic:

> We differ from our closest known relatives in numerous features of the skull and of the postcranial skeleton, in important features of brain growth, and almost certainly in critical features of internal brain organization as well. These differences exist on an unusual scale.... We evidently came by our unusual anatomical structure and capacities very recently: There is certainly no evidence to support the notion that we gradually became what we inherently are over an extended period, in either the physical or the intellectual sense.[2]

Human Exceptionalism

IN HIS groundbreaking Gifford Lecture of 1914, Arthur Balfour identified what he called "inevitable beliefs" or what elsewhere he describes as "departments of human interests," such as emotions, beauty, and morality.[3] What Balfour labeled inevitable beliefs, for lack of a generic name in 1914, is what Wesley J. Smith calls human exceptionalism a century later.[4] Human exceptionalism is the belief that the human person is different from all other animals not merely in degree but also in kind.

Naturally the perspective of Balfour and Smith could not go unchallenged. Professor Craig Stanford of the University of Southern California leads the charge in claiming that, on the contrary, the difference between animals and human beings is only in degrees and not in kind. A scrutiny of his argument suggests that Stanford knows his animals well. What is doubtful is whether his knowledge of the human is as thorough.

A Wikipedia article claims that human exceptionalism is "often argued on religious grounds."[5] But the evidence presented here is scientific, not religious. Science favors a view of humans as exceptional.

Professor Jonathan Marks, a biological anthropologist at the University of North Carolina at Charlotte, avers,

> It is not that difficult to tell a human from an ape, after all. The human is the one walking, talking, sweating, praying, building, reading, trading, crying, dancing, writing, cooking, joking, working, decorating, shaving, driving a car, or playing football.... and of course, our cognitive communication abilities and the productive anatomies of our tongue and throat are all dead giveaways.[6]

Molecular biologist Ann Gauger concurs. "It is true that we share a lot in common with animals," Gauger writes. "It is true that we have DNA, RNA, and proteins in common, that we have mitochondria and organelles in common, that we have brains and bones in common. But we also have many things that we do not have in common with animals."[7] She goes on to list such things. Unmistakably, they are gifts, attesting to the attributes of the human which Balfour said do not have a generic name. Gauger writes:

For example, our ability to think abstractly about *things not necessary for survival* is amazing. In fact, spending the time to learn to do them well is likely to hinder survival (sorry, savants!).... We write motets, we calculate equations that take us into space, we write jazz songs about flying to the moon and sing them at age 7, we plan ways to terraform Mars (no chimp does that!) and study Greek plays by people long dead.

We use voice dictation software that others of us have made, that is sometimes almost poetic in its interpretation of what we just said, in fact, so poetic that we can't tell what it was supposed to be. No chimp does that.

We build incredible cities. We do horrible things well beyond what animals are capable of to each other. We have language, that wonderful, marvelous, treacherous gift. We have music, that powerful, glorious, dangerous gift. And we have art, that beautiful, transcendent, painful gift. All these gifts are things that animals don't have. They are qualitatively, not just quantitatively, different, and they are well past anything that could have evolved.[8]

Society

BALFOUR RECOGNIZES some similarities between the society of bees and "the lifelong fidelity of the parent birds in certain species" on the one hand, and human society on the other. First, there is a striking similarity in the observable division of labor in beehive as well as in human community. Secondly, there is observable organized effort towards an end which is other and greater than the individual good of any single member of the beehive.

Nevertheless, there are chasms of differences between the beehive and the lifelong fidelity of the parent birds in certain species on the one hand and human society on the other. For one thing, humans are capable of assessing and choosing between alternative plans. For another, each human must weigh the individual benefits to him against the general benefits to society, which is something animals and insects cannot do.

Morality

Further, Balfour sees immense differences between instincts in animals and morality or ethics in human society. They are observable

> in the egoistic as in the non-egoistic region of ethics. Ideals of conduct, the formulation of ends, judgments of their relative worth, actions based on principles, deliberate choice between alternative policies, the realised distinction between the self and other personalities or other centres of feeling—all these are involved in developed morality, while in animal ethics they exist not at all, or only in the most rudimentary forms.[9]

Political scientist John West points out the unimaginable society that would emerge were the distinction between right and wrong, true or false, obliterated:

> After all, if human behaviors and beliefs are ultimately the products of natural selection, then all such behaviors and beliefs must be equally preferable. The same Darwinian process that produces the maternal instinct also produces infanticide. The same Darwinian process that generates love also brings forth sadism. The same Darwinian process that inspires courage also spawns cowardice. Hence, the logical result of a Darwinian account of morality is not so much of immorality as relativism.[10]

Instinct is based on or conceded to biology, but the human sense of right and wrong is rooted in something else or somewhere else—in the transcendent. This is not to deny that human beings have instinct in addition to morality; but the two are different and are put to different functions by human beings.

The Intellect

And then there arises the question of the intellect and knowledge. There is a limit to the scope of empiricism, that theory which states that knowledge comes only or primarily from that which our senses experience. As Balfour perceptively clarifies in his Gifford Lectures, "When all had been done that could be done to systematise our ordinary modes of experimental inference, the underlying problem of knowledge still remained unsolved."[11]

C. S. Lewis, the Anglo-Irish World War I veteran who rose to become an accomplished philosopher and professor later in life, did not locate the human mind and rationality in natural selection. With characteristic sarcasm, he taunts Social Darwinism as follows: "If my own mind is a product of the irrational [Charles Darwin's randomness]... how shall I trust my mind when it tells me about Evolution?"[12]

The findings of Wilder Penfield (1891–1976), founding director of Montreal Neurological Institute and Hospital, who expanded brain surgery's methods and techniques, including mapping the functions of various regions of the brain such as the cortical homunculus, confirms the argument Lewis makes in his rhetorical question. Penfield is known for making many scientific contributions involving neural stimulation and as the pioneer in surgery for epilepsy. What is perhaps less widely known is his conversion from materialism (the false belief that physical matter is the only and fundamental reality) to dualism (the belief that there is a part of the human that is not composed of physical matter).

Neurosurgeon Michael Egnor explains Penfield's three lines of reasoning, which changed Penfield's mind about the nature of humans. First, although Penfield performed surgery on more than a thousand epileptic patients, and though he mapped more than a thousand brains with hundreds of individual stimulations of the brain surface, "he never once stimulated the power of reason. He never stimulated the intellect. He never stimulated a person to do calculus or to think of an abstract concept like justice or mercy."[13] Thus, as Egnor puts it, "Penfield said hey, if the brain is the source of abstract thought, once in a while, putting an electrical current on some part of the cortex, I ought to get an abstract thought. He never, ever did. So he said that the obvious explanation for that is that abstract thought doesn't come from the brain."[14]

Second, although the foremost authority on epilepsy in his day, Penfield "never found any seizure that had intellectual content." Egnor explains:

Seizures never involved abstract reasoning.... Nobody ever had a calculus seizure. Nobody ever had a seizure where they couldn't stop doing arithmetic. Or couldn't stop doing logic. And he said, why is that? If arithmetic and logic and all that abstract thought come from the brain, every once in a while you ought to get a seizure that makes it happen. So he asked rhetorically, why are there no intellectual seizures? His answer was, because the intellect doesn't come from the brain.[15]

Third, Penfield experimented during brain surgery. Keep in mind that brain tissue itself doesn't have pain sensors (which explains why neurosurgeons can cut on brain tissue without causing the patient discomfort). Penfield would ask a patient to move his arm, and sometimes Penfield would stimulate the brain himself to make the arm move. The patients always knew which was happening. Egnor says, "He couldn't stimulate the will. He could never trick the patients into thinking it was them doing it. He said, the patients always retained a correct sense of agency. They always know if they did it or if he did it."[16]

Thus Penfield came to the firm conclusion that "the intellect and the will are not from the brain."[17] Penfield thought that consciousness depended on "electrochemical mechanisms within the brainstem," but that consciousness functioned "beyond the laws of physics."[18] Moreover, Penfield did not doubt the existence of the human soul, though he questioned whether science had the equipment to establish its existence.[19]

Love

LOVE IS also impossible for materialist science to explain. Miriam Frankel, the science editor at *The Conversation*, asked neuroscientist Parashkev Nachev to write an article about love. His resulting article, titled "Love: Is It Just a Fleeting High Fuelled by Brain Chemicals," presents the interesting finding that while "sex pheromones, chemicals designed to broadcast reproductive availability to others... play an important role in insect communication, there is very little evidence that they even exist in humans."[20]

Nachev further explains that when the prime candidate, oxytocin (known as the "bonding hormone"), is blocked in the monogamous prairie vole, the prairie vole becomes less affectionate towards its mate. The same test performed on humans produces less dramatic results. "So," he says, "oxytocin is far from proven to be essential to love. Even if we could identify such a substance, any message—chemical or otherwise—needs a recipient. So where is the letterbox of love in the brain? And how is the identity of the 'chosen one' conveyed, given that no single molecule could possibly encode it?"[21]

He then says, "Do we simply need more experiments? Yes, is usually the scientist's answer, but here that assumes love is simple enough to be captured by a mechanistic description. And that is extremely unlikely."[22]

Our Answer

ARE WE merely highly evolved animals? No. We have seen there are features of the human person not found in the other living organisms. These features are ones human society cannot do without, without destroying itself. And those features are demonstrably not rooted in evolution. They are exterior to biology; they are rooted in the Transcendent.

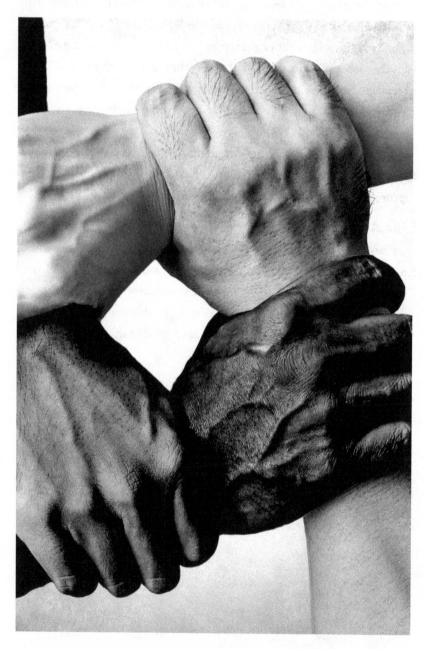

Figure 11.1. We are all part of the same human race.

11. Are There Foundational Differences?

Now we reach the crux of the matter. Biologically speaking, are there foundational differences between blacks and whites that might justify the belief that blacks are more primitive, less highly evolved humans?

It will surely come as no surprise that the answer is "no." Scientific advances of the twentieth and twenty-first centuries have shown no biogenetically distinct races. Rather, "human physical variations do not fit a 'racial' model. Instead, human physical variations tend to overlap."[1]

No Genetic Differences

Science has tried to distinguish "race" on the basis of blood types and other genetic markers. However:

> When scientists tried to show a correlation of blood group patterns with the conventional races, they found none. While populations differed in their blood group patterns, in such features as the frequencies of A, B, and O types, no evidence was found to document race distinctions. As knowledge of human heredity expanded, other genetic markers of difference were sought, but these also failed to neatly separate humanity into races. Most differences are expressed in subtle gradations over wide geographic space, not in abrupt changes from one "race" to another. Moreover, not all groups within a large "geographic race" share the same patterns of genetic features. The internal variations within races have proved to be greater than those between races.[2]

Nor did DNA genetic analysis help:

There are no genes that can identify distinct groups that accord with the conventional race categories. In fact, DNA analyses have proved that all humans have much more in common, genetically, than they have differences. The genetic difference between any two humans is less than 1 percent. Moreover, geographically widely separated populations vary from one another in only about 6 to 8 percent of their genes. Because of the overlapping of traits that bear no relationship to one another (such as skin colour and hair texture) and the inability of scientists to cluster peoples into discrete racial packages, modern researchers have concluded that the concept of race has no biological validity.[3]

No Intellectual Differences

NOR CAN intelligence be used to divide humans into separate races. Americans in particular once relied heavily on Intelligence Quotient tests, and indeed "on average, blacks did less well than whites on IQ tests. But the tests also revealed that the disadvantaged people of all races do worse on IQ tests than do the privileged."[4]

Further undermining the connection between IQ and race was the work of Otto Klineberg, who in the 1930s demonstrated that blacks in four northern states outperformed whites in four southern states and thus became instrumental in furthering desegregation.[5] It would seem that other factors—family expectations, exposure to various cultural experiences, and so forth—affect performance on IQ tests more than does the color of one's skin. As Rutledge M. Dennis notes, "Such studies and debates reveal far more about those proposing and advocating racial arguments than about the groups toward whom they are directed."[6]

"No Biological Basis for Races"

ONE OF the most vocal proponents of dividing humanity into races was Ernst Haeckel of Jena University, Germany. Haeckel, an ardent admirer of Charles Darwin, first proposed dividing humanity into ten and, later, twelve races. He argued that Caucasians were the most intelligent and blacks best adapted to the tropics, and promoted scientific racism leading to eugenics, anti-Semitism, involuntary sterilizations, racial wars, the racial policy of Nazi Germany, xenophobia, apartheid, and so on.

Thus it is of great significance that it was at the same university, the citadel where Haeckel wreaked havoc against humanity, that the German Zoological Society chose to hold its 112th Annual Meeting in August 2019, at which it co-issued the historic Jena Declaration with Jena University—as if the university were washing its hands of the inhumanity that had been hatched and perpetuated under its name.

The Jena Declaration notes, first, that "the notion that different groups of people differ in value preceded supposedly scientific work on the subject. The primarily biological justification for defining groups of humans as races—for example based on the colour of their skin or eyes, or the shape of their skulls—has led to the persecution, enslavement, and slaughter of millions of people."[7]

Secondly, the Declaration says that "there is no biological basis for races, and there has never been one. The concept of race is the result of racism, not its prerequisite."

The Declaration then takes aim specifically at Haeckel:

The position of human groups in... [Haeckel's] tree of life was based on arbitrarily selected characteristics such as skin colour or hair structure, presented from a phylogenetic point of view. This resulted in these people being viewed in a particular sequence, which implied that some groups had higher or lower status on biological grounds than others.

Further, the Declaration addresses Ernst Mayr's work, which was akin to that of Ernst Haeckel, but focusing on geography and taxonomic difference to divide human populations. The Jena Declaration is emphatic that "determining which taxonomic difference or genetic differentiation would be sufficient to distinguish races or subspecies is completely arbitrary," thereby rendering the concept of races/subspecies in biology purely a construct of the human mind.

Superficial Differences

This does not, of course, mean that there are no differences among individual members of the human race. Some of us are lighter in skin, others darker. But

> external features such as skin colour, which are used to classify types of people, are an extremely superficial and changeable biological adaptation to existing local conditions. Skin colour alone has frequently changed in the course of human migrations and has become darker and lighter according to local solar radiation or diet....
>
> The linking of features such as skin colour with characteristics or even supposedly genetically fixed personality traits and behaviours, as was done in the heyday of anthropological racism, has now been soundly refuted. To use such arguments today as seemingly scientific is both wrong and malicious. There is also no scientifically proven connection between intelligence and geographical origin, but there is a clear connection with social background. Here too, racism in the form of exclusion and discrimination creates supposed races.[8]

The Christian missionary Dr. Walter Miller noted long ago that skin is merely superficial. Miller spent fifty-two years practicing medicine while building one of the best schools in Northern Nigeria, building a Christian congregation, and at the same time translating the Bible into Hausa, approximately fifty years before one of theirs translated the Koran into Hausa. After thirty-six years of mending the broken bodies of Christians, Muslims, and pagans, the majority of whom were Hausa and Fulani, Miller was as categorical as he could be on the matter of the European-African superiority-inferiority binary: "It is not claimed that there is a difference in the red corpuscles of the blood of white and black. Difference in the pigment cells of the skin is a much more serious matter apparently!"[9]

The Jena Declaration does not suggest there are no variations in skin color, only that these do not define races. The Jena Declaration also does not "mean that there is no genetic differentiation along a geographical gradient. However, the taxonomic evaluation of this differentiation (as race or subspecies, or not) is arbitrary. This is even more strongly the case for humans, where the greatest genetic differences are found within a population and not between populations."

Thus, the Jena Declaration concludes, "Let us ensure that people are never again discriminated against on specious biological grounds and remind ourselves and others that it is racism that has created races and that zoology/anthropology has played an inglorious part in producing supposedly biological justifications."

There is no scientific evidence of any difference between the foundational building blocks of Europeans and black Africans, contrary to Social Darwinist propaganda.

Late to the Party

THE JENA Declaration, while important, was grounded in an understanding long obvious to those who hold to biblical principles. According to scripture, all humans are made in the image of God, and all are thus equally worthy of dignity and respect.[10] Finally "science" acknowledges what Christians knew long ago.

And let there be no mistake: the Social Darwinist attack on "inferior" people was also and congruently an attack on Judeo-Christian ethics. Bernard Lightman points out, "Darwin attempted in *Origin* to secularize nature"[11] and Sharon Kingsland notes, "Darwin's theory was mainly an argument against 'special creation,' the doctrine that species originated suddenly and by divine intervention."[12] Darwinism rejects the Genesis creation story; the Judeo-Christian belief in the supernatural; the distinction between humans and other animals; body-soul dualism; and the Christian portrayal of death as an enemy, contrary to the Darwinist view that death is a force for progress.

Further, Darwinism and Christianity are antithetical not only in what they hold to be true about the human person, but in what they hold to be true about the origin of morality. Whereas Judeo-Christian thought posits a transcendent Being from whom principles of right and wrong derive, Darwinism posits that "ethics [are] not timeless truths transcending historical epochs" but are only "relative to the individual's fitness in the Darwinian struggle for existence."[13] Thus Francis Galton—Darwin's cousin who pioneered eugenics, the pseudo-scientific and political movement of controlling who becomes a parent as a way of improving the hereditary qualities of a race or class—"imagined a perfect society in which human breeding would be taken as seriously as the breeding of domestic animals, a society in which the ideal of 'race improvement' would become the basis for a new ethics that would supplant Christianity."[14]

Richard Weikart explains that Haeckel "was notorious for his hostility to Christianity and his rejection of Judeo-Christian ethics, and he was not alone among Darwinists," many of whom waged a "campaign against Judeo-Christian religious and ethical thought."[15] As Darwinists in Germany were prepared to make clear, the "ethics of eugenics derived from the theory of evolution and selection explicitly oppose the Christian ethic of the individual."[16] One prominent Darwinist wrote in 1894 that "whatever promotes the progress of the species is morally good, and whatever leads to weak or sick individuals is morally bad, despite what Christianity or any other system of ethics may say."[17]

Such different views of humanity and human origins are irreconcilable.[18]

It is thus, then, no wonder that proponents of Social Darwinism—such as Frederick Lugard in Northern Nigeria—sought and still seek to exclude Christians and Christianity from their domain. And it is no wonder that contemporary proponents of Darwinism continue to paint Christianity as the enemy of science, when in fact it is Darwinism that is at odds both with science and with principles that would, if so allowed, promote harmony amongst all so-called races, as well as amongst individuals.

Figure 12.1. Stele of the ancient African kingdom of Axum, fourth century AD.

12. The Not-So-Dark Continent

DARWIN WAS WRONG ABOUT HUMAN ORIGINS; HIS FOLLOWERS were wrong about so-called inferior races being fundamentally different biologically from the so-called superior races. But we still must consider the separate category of ethnicity, which has to do not with the fundamental building blocks of biology, nor with superficials such as skin color, but with geography—with the cultural traits and common history of a given people in a certain part of the world. Are the people of some regions more evolutionarily advanced than peoples of other geographical regions? Does knowledge, progress, and virtue always flow from the North to the South? Frederick Lugard and his cohorts believed so. For example, Charles Temple saw a connection between "geographical conditions" and "grades of civilisation." Hence, "from the basis of his Social Darwinist assumptions, Temple argues that the behaviour, customs and institutions developed by Native communities generally correspond to their stage of development."[1]

Most assuredly, this is not so! Many times knowledge, virtue, and progress have flowed northwardly from southern regions. Indeed, when Egypt was a world power—before the era of Arab occupation—knowledge flowed not just northward but in every direction.

Morality

CONSIDER THAT there are cultures in all geographical regions where morality is inferior (often because Christianity has not reached them or where, as in Europe and the United States, it is now in decline). Virtues and vices are found across all geographies and ethnic groups.

On the one hand, Resident G. Webster, of Yola Province, documented among other things that the Mumbake of Yola Province were a people among whom "murder was unknown."[2] Of what northern nation can that be said?

On the other hand, in 1907, the Sudan United Mission newsletter (*Lightbearer*) announced the arrival of Joseph Baker, the first black SUM missionary to the field, and asked his first impression at Ibi, a center of trade where SUM maintained a station. Baker lamented, "Away from public opinion, away with moral restraint, would seem to be the motto of a good many men in this part of the world. Licentiousness is the fashion out here, both with white and coloured men."[3]

Likewise Herbert Tugwell, Anglican Bishop of Lagos, who lived in Lagos and observed firsthand the behavior of fellow Europeans in coastal Lagos for thirteen years, declared, "The death of Europeans was by no means always due to malaria alone: 75% was due to the sins of the victims."[4] Even Flora Lugard noted in 1905 that "the conduct of all Europeans towards the black women was as discreditable as it was injurious to themselves."[5]

By comparison, Thomas Bowen, having lived among the Yoruba for many years, declared in 1856 that "although the women do not marry till they are eighteen or twenty years of age, I have never known a case of an illegitimate child."[6] Further, the Tangale had no venereal disease, whereas the Spanish spread syphilis far and wide.

Thus it cannot be said that people of one geography are naturally more moral than those of another. The case of Europeans calling African savages, or stigmatizing Africa as "the Dark Continent" is a case of the pot calling the kettle black. Some cultures are more immoral than others, but it is not because they are lower on the evolutionary ladder. If that were the case, then surely contemporary Northern societies would be at the very bottom of the ladder.

Economy and Technology

LIKEWISE THERE are cultures in all geographies where material or economic progress lags. Such disparities are not due to any inherent differences among people per se, but to other external forces such as a lack of natural resources, a dearth of education, corrupt political leadership, or what have you.

In many cases the achievements of those in supposedly inferior geographical regions have been overlooked, misunderstood, or willfully obscured.

Alice Gorman, speaking of Australia's aborigines, explains:

In 1859, Charles Darwin published *On the Origin of Species*. He proposed that animal species changed over time through natural selection, sometimes called "survival of the fittest."

Applied to human societies, Darwin's theory gave rise to a race-based notion of "progress"—with the white, Christian male at the pinnacle of human evolution.

American anthropologist Lewis Morgan, in his 1877 book *Ancient Society*, argued that all human populations passed through the stages of "Savagery, through Barbarism to Civilization." Stone tool technology, he argued, was a feature of savagery.

The stage was set to construct Indigenous people as living representatives of the past who had never evolved. This was no longer an analogy, but a judgement.

In the 19th and 20th centuries, these ideas were put to sinister use as European nations expanded their colonies in Indigenous lands.[7]

Once it had been determined that a certain geographical group was "inferior," habits and technologies associated with that group likewise were considered "inferior." For instance, for the Aborigines,

The use of stone tools thus became a liability.... [Yet] contrary to popular belief, stone tool technology is not simple. It is highly skilled, requiring knowledge of geomorphology, geology, fracture mechanics and the thermal properties of stone. Thousands of archaeologists studying stone tools can only approximate the complexity of a science that enabled Aboriginal people to survive and thrive through some of the most challenging environmental changes in human history.

Stone tools are still being made and used, and not just by Indigenous people. In 1975 the archaeologist Don Crabtree underwent surgery with obsidian scalpels he had manufactured himself. Obsidian blades cause less tissue damage than surgical steel knives, and the wounds heal more quickly. Surgeons still use them. Stone working is one of the most successful technologies used by humans and their ancestors—from 3.3 million years ago to the present day.[8]

Something "different" from the European norm need not be "worse."

Empires

According to Lugard, "Africa has been justly termed 'the Dark Continent,' for the secrets of its peoples, its lakes, and mountains and rivers, have remained undisclosed not merely to modern civilisation, but through all the ages of which history has any record."[9] Lugard also wrote, "The history of these peoples of tropical Africa... has during the ages prior to the advent of the European explorers some sixty years ago been an impenetrable mystery.... Unlike the ancient civilisations of Asia and South America, the former inhabitants of Africa have left no monuments and no records other than rude drawings on rocks like those of Neolithic man."[10]

Assigning rude drawings on rocks, whatever that means, as the only legacy of an entire continent, says so much more about Frederick Lugard than about Africa and Africans. His ethnocentrism here is on full display, as is his foolishness and pride. He was not a historian, nor was he mindful of African history even after spending forty years there.

Let us briefly review the achievements of some ancient African empires.

Egypt

Egyptian civilization rose according to many historians by around 3000 BC, with Nubia at an early stage, and the Axumite Kingdom later. Egypt is justly famous for the pyramids; the solar calendar; irrigation;

early forms of paper; a form of writing based on hieroglyphics; detailed knowledge of anatomy, surgery, philosophy, and mathematics. Indeed the Greek mathematician Archimedes is thought to have studied in Egypt, as did Pythagoras.

Kush

According to Sophia Carvalho and Clive Harris, the history of Kush is closely intertwined with northern Egyptian Nubia.[11] In fact, it was formerly part of Egypt, but it later gained its freedom and forged its own path of development and greatness. The Kushites were known for "impressive architecture, irrigation systems, scripts and iron industry," and a twenty-three symbol alphabet that replaced Egyptian hieroglyphics. The Kushite society was highly literate.[12]

Axum

The kingdom of Axum was located primarily in Northeast Africa. After his conversion to the Christian faith, King Ezana of Axum made Christianity the state religion eight years before Constantine did the same in Europe in AD 337. King Negus Armah protected Mohammed, the prophet of Islam, his family, and the followers with him from the persecution of Arab pagans. Although it was in Kush that the twenty-three symbol alphabet was developed, it was in the Axumite period that it was internationalized. Christian missionaries to Armenia in central Europe and Georgia in eastern Europe used the Ge'ez alphabet as the template for Armenian and Georgian scripts.

After Axum transformed itself into the Ethiopian State under the Zagwe dynasty around the middle of the eleventh century, this empire constructed "a dozen wonderful churches hewn from sandstone rock at Roha/Lalibela by Prince Lalibela who reigned from 1167 to 1207."[13]

Nok

There was a certain ancient people group occupying the region south of the colonial Plateau Province to the north, and the Niger and Benue basins to the south, but whose name scholars have yet to determine.

They are tentatively identified as Nok, a place in the Southern Kaduna district in Nigeria's Middle Belt. The exact period of this empire's origin is unclear, but its demise occurred around AD 200. Nok is identified with "astonishingly sophisticated artifacts." Nok used iron for ploughs and weapons. It produced sculptures from fired clay or terracotta, and the sculpted figures are adorned with "elaborately designed hair styles and jewellery and reveal a strong devotion to beauty and body ornamentation."[14] Its artistic forms are similar to Yoruba art.

Ghana

The old Ghana Empire integrated contemporary Mali, with its territory reaching as far as Mauritania, with parts of Senegal and Guinea. It reached its zenith in AD 1076. Note that Ghana thus was an empire when England was under French colonial rule. Ghana featured homes "built out of stone with glass windows with an upstairs and downstairs floor, sculptures and pictures on walls, princes with hair plaited with gold, and dogs wearing collars of silver and gold." Ghana's wealth came from international trade, and the government taxed both imports and exports of goods. According to Carvalho and Harris, "Ghana also produced and traded metal goods, cotton cloth and copper. They sold their high quality leather to Moroccans who then sold it on to Europeans as 'Moroccan leather.'"[15] Further, "cheques were an accepted method of payment in tenth century Ghana," which also had "a royal court of justice, with lawyers and scholars."[16]

Mali-Manding

According to Carvalho and Harris, "Many people tend to think of Mali solely as a Muslim state, and begin its history with its first Muslim king. Mali was however a kingdom for two hundred and fifty years before Islam was adopted as the state religion."[17]

Further, the medieval Arab historian al-Umari wrote that a ruler of the Mali empire, while visiting Cairo, reported that his predecessor "did not believe that it was impossible to discover the furthest limit of the Atlantic Ocean and wished vehemently to do so." When the expedition he sent out failed, with only a single ship returning and nothing to show for the effort, the sultan himself "got ready 2,000 ships... and embarked on the Atlantic Ocean with his men. That was the last we saw of him and all those who were with him."[18] This was 181 years before Christopher Columbus reached the Americas.[19] Historian Michael Gomez weighs the evidence pro and con for this story. In the end he leaves the question undecided, but he notes that "even if mythical, to speak of such a voyage reflects a certain aggressiveness, a kind of restlessness on the part of a growing central authority fueled by unchecked territorial expansion. A vast realm had allegedly been formed," one reaching Ghana and the Atlantic in the west and the land of Takrur in the east, an impressive breadth of imperial expansion with support among other historians of the period.[20]

Kanem-Bornu

The Kanem-Bornu Empire in the area known as present day Chare rose at about the same time as the Mali-Manding Empire. The area was a temporary stop-over for about two to three centuries for the Berber from North Africa who rejected and fled Islamic compulsion before some of them finally settled in Borguland in present-day Nigeria in the eleventh century.

Edris, "one of the greatest of the kings of Bornu, was making gunpowder for the muskets of his army at a period contemporary with Queen Elizabeth."[21] Further, "You may remember that on the accession of Queen Elizabeth in 1588 the English arsenals contained chiefly bows and arrows." It may be of some surprise that these statements were made by Flora Lugard.[22]

Songhai

After the fall of Mali-Manding empire, the Songhai empire gained prominence for about a century. It was in alliance with Queen Elizabeth I against Spain. In the sixteenth century Leo Africanus, a German traveler, came to Timbuktu and wrote that he witnessed "many judges, doctors, and clerics here, all receiving good salaries from King Askia

Mohammed of the State of Songhai. He pays great respect to men of learning. There is a great demand for books, and more profit is made from the trade in books than from any other line of business."[23]

Other well documented African empires include Benin, Oyo-Yoruba (which owes nothing to Islam), Zimbabwe, Azania, Engaruka in East Africa, and the Rift Valley near the Kenya-Tanzanian border.[24]

Achievements

Now LET us move from empires to a consideration of specific achievements.

Textiles

In 1912, none other than Charles Temple expressed his amazement that "the imported [Manchester] cloth is not nearly so durable as that made locally" in Northern Nigeria.[25] His wife, in her survey of Nigerian textiles, likewise noted its high quality.[26] So did Constance Larymore, who carefully detailed the skill and enterprise involved in dyeing, weaving, and selling various woven articles.[27]

Canon Charles Robinson, Lecturer in Hausa in the University of Cambridge, noted when he was on a language proficiency sojourn in Kano in 1895,

> At the time of the Norman conquest of England trade was being conducted in the Kano market amidst surroundings closely resembling those that we now see. Kano would then have furnished better-made cloth than any to be found in England at that time. The really unique interest, however, attaching to this market arises from the fact that it forms the centre of a native civilisation which has been attained with very little aid from outside sources and with none at all from Europe.[28]

William MacGregor, the Lagos Governor, and daily Greek New Testament reader, said before the Royal African Institute in London in June 1904: "It is confidently expected that in the near future cotton will become an important export from this province. The cotton plant is indigenous there. It has been cultivated, spun, and woven from time immemorial all over Yorubaland. Some of the native kinds are of good quality, and seem to stand the summer drought better than imported varieties."[29]

Allister Hinds notes:

As early as the fourteenth century textile productions systems in the north of the Niger-Benue confluence were linked to Muslim trading networks. By the nineteenth century, important centers of textile manufacture existed in Kano, Bida and Ilorin in the Sokoto Caliphate; in Yoruba areas such as Yagba; and in Benin. At these centers production was highly organized and a consistently high standard of cloth was produced.[30]

It is clear from the foregoing that, first, textile business was part of pre-colonial economy in most parts of Northern Nigeria. Second, it ranged from the international level such as in the case of Kano, to the inter-ethnic in the case of Burra and the Waja, to less ambitious aims such as for local needs. This is a challenge to the familiar rhetoric of nude savages.

Were some Africans nude or only partially clothed? Of course. Christian modesty may disapprove of nudity, but in secular terms can immodesty be called uncivilized? If so, then the streets of Europe and the United States grow less civilized day by day. Nor do these northern countries have the logical reasons for immodesty that southern countries of past history had.

Consider the Bafum Katse of Muri Province (Sudan). A European visitor during the era of the Lugards deemed them "primitive" because they were nude, and yet in the same breath praised their architecture, furniture, government, near self-sufficient economy, peacefulness, and cleanliness.[31] Did this visitor ask why they were nude? No! He simply put them in the "primitive" box because of it.

Or consider the nude Tangale people. Gordon Beacham, one of the first two Westerners—both missionaries—to live and work among the Tangale of Gombe Division, learned that the Tera and Waja, Tangale's neighbors, thought "weaving second in importance to farming" and routinely teased the Tangale on their decision to go naked. Beacham explained, "if the Tera or Waja man ridicules the Tangale on account of his nakedness, the Tangale will retort, that the other only wears cloth to save taking a bath."[32] Of course, the Tera and the Waja could make more money if the Tangale patronized them, thereby saving the former the hazards of long distance travelling to sell their textile wares.

Beacham inquired and discovered that the Tangale "have not always lived so, for they themselves and their neighboring Moslems, who fought them unsuccessfully in days gone by, testify that when they migrated from the north to their present location, they wore clothing, but when they began their warfare, they discarded their clothes as hindrances in flight through the bush."[33] They were not always nude! It was a strategic decision of warfare. To interpret their nakedness as evidence of how little they had progressed on the contrived evolutionary ladder is neither anthropology nor science.

And recall, further, that the nude Tangale had no venereal disease!

Astronomy

The ruins of an astronomical observatory dating to 300 BC have been found at Namoratunga in Kenya.[34] Moreover, Nabta Playa in the Nubian Desert holds a stone circle far older than Stonehenge. The stones "aligned to Arcturus, Sirius, and Alpha Centauri" in 4800 BC. "That makes it the oldest astronomical site we've ever discovered," says J. McKim Malville, an expert on archaeoastronomy.[35]

There is "convincing evidence that the scholars of Timbuktu knew a lot more than their counterparts in Europe." Indeed, "in the fifteenth century in Timbuktu the mathematicians knew about the rotation of the planets, knew about the details of the eclipse, they knew things which we had to wait for... almost 200 years to know in Europe when Galileo and Copernicus came up with these same calculations and were given a very hard time for it."[36]

Mathematics

The famous Fibonacci sequence is so called because of its popularization by the Italian Leonardo Bonacci (filius Bonacci, or Fibonacci for

Fine

short, meaning "son of Bonacci"). However, although Fibonacci introduced these beautiful and useful numbers to Europe, he did not discover this important mathematical concept. Rather, he learned it upon visiting North Africa.[37] The sequence is, in fact, an integral part of African design. The Fibonacci curve is found, for instance, in the layout of an ancient palace compound in Cameroon.

A research team with the CSDT (Culturally Situated Design Tools) notes:

> Anthropologists have observed that many Indigenous African societies created fractals in their architecture, textiles, sculpture, art, and religion. This was not simply unconscious or intuitive, as Africans linked these designs to concepts such as recursion and scaling. Why did Africans focus so much on fractal designs while other groups did more with Euclidian geometry? Every culture makes use of certain geometric design themes. Native Americans, for example, made four-fold symmetry central to their designs. The African focus on fractals emphasizes their own cultural priorities.[38]

Architecture

The use of mathematical fractals and intricate designs are not the only matters of architectural interest in African history. To give but a very few examples, Sudan in the medieval period had churches, cathedrals, monasteries, and castles, and their ruins still exist today. These buildings feature window glass.

In the ninth century AD Sudanese dwellings featured bathrooms and piped-in water. Likewise, the Kenya city of Gedi had piped-in water by the fourteenth or fifteenth century. Gedi of this time had a palace, private houses, a Great Mosque, and seven smaller mosques. Chinese records of the sixteenth century AD note that Mogadishu had houses reaching four or five stories high.

And a traveler in 1331 AD called the Tanzanian city of Kilwa "one of the most beautiful and well-constructed cities in the world."[39]

Steel

East Africans have been making steel for more than 1,500 years:

Assistant Professor of Anthropology Peter Schmidt and Professor of Engineering Donald H. Avery have found as long as 2,000 years ago Africans living on the western shores of Lake Victoria had produced carbon steel in preheated forced draft furnaces, a method that was technologically more sophisticated than any developed in Europe until the mid-nineteenth century.[40]

These were the Hayas of what is today Tanzania. As John H. Lienhard notes, "Today, ancient African ingenuity gives us steel."[41]

Surgery

Surgeons in pre-colonial Uganda performed autopsies and caesarean operations routinely and effectively, using antiseptics, anesthetics, and cautery iron. The *Edinburgh Medical Journal* in 1884 wrote of one Ugandan caesarean, saying, "The whole conduct of the operation... suggests a skilled long-practiced surgical team at work conducting a well-tried and familiar operation with smooth efficiency."[42]

Furthermore, it is relevant to point out that the King of Kaiama in Borguland performed a surgical operation on Frederick Lugard in 1894, removing a poisoned arrow from his skull.

At that time, Lugard was the commandant of the Royal Niger Company mercenary army. Lugard failed to document this pivotal occasion in his life, perhaps because it would have raised European opinions of the African and undermined his Social Darwinist "primitive savage" narrative. While Lugard omitted the surgical operation from all his records, the Borgu did not blot it out of their history.[43]

Medicine

In her recent book, *Secret Cures of Slaves: People, Plants, and Medicine in the Eighteenth-Century Atlantic*, Londa Schiebinger, professor of history of science at Stanford University, devotes space to African contributions to medical knowledge and practice. Her examples include that of Alexander J. Alexander, a Scottish planter who arrived in 1773 at his extensive plantation in Grenada, a small island south of Barbados, just off the coast of South America, from which he had been absent for quite some time. There he found thirty-two of his slaves afflicted with yaws and confined to the plantation hospital; some of them had been there for years. Yaws is a bacterial infection that flourishes in humid, tropical climates. It produces terrible ulcers and crippling pain, particularly in the hands and feet. However, Enlightenment doctors assumed yaws to be a venereal disease, and so Alexander's "surgeon employed standard mercurial treatment, which, when taken over several years… left slaves' health 'broken.'"[44]

According to Alexander's letters, which later were published in the *Medical and Philosophical Commentaries*, he looked for a "Negro who understood the Method of treatment in their [sic] own Country." Alexander put two yawey slaves under the care of the slave doctor and four yawey patients under the care of his own surgeon. Their treatments differed. Alexander reported that the black doctor sweated his patients "powerfully," having them stand twice a day "in a Cask where there is a little fire in a pot." He increased the sweat by giving them decoctions of two woods that Alexander identified as *bois royale* and *bois fer*. In addition, the unnamed man applied to their sores an ointment of iron rust and lime juice.[45]

The European surgeon, by contrast, treated his four patients with drugs to induce sweats. To their sores he applied various noxious caustics including *sacharum saturni* (sugar of lead), green vitriol, antimony, and corrosive sublimate. These treatments caused the slaves much pain.

What was the outcome? The slave's patients were cured within a fortnight; the surgeon's patients were not. Alexander, a man of science, consequently gave the man of African origins four more patients, who were also quickly cured. Thereafter he put the slave in charge of all yaws patients in his plantation hospital, and at the end of two months all but about ten of the original thirty-two had been cured.[46]

Thereafter Alexander's confidence in the enslaved man grew, and Alexander turned to him for other cures as well. What was conspicuously missing in Alexander's accounts, unfortunately, was the name of the Africa slave doctor who taught Europe how to cure yaws.

Commerce

What of business acumen? Did Africa lag behind? No! As has been mentioned in passing elsewhere, trading, business, and commerce took place long before Europeans arrived. The Hausa were the most travelled people in pre-colonial West Africa, creating trade routes in different parts of western Africa long before the advent of colonial rule. Ghana, as we have seen, grew wealthy through international trade. There were many forms of production, trade, and commerce amongst the peoples of Africa.

Literacy

In the sixteenth century a West African scholar in Timbuktu wrote that his library was smaller than the libraries of his friends—he had only 1,600 books.[47] A European visitor at that time noted, "There is a great demand for books, and more profit is made from the trade in books than from any other line of business."[48]

Nor were books uncommon elsewhere in Africa. The medieval Nubian kingdom contained archives of thousands of documents written in Meroitic, Latin, Coptic, Greek, Old Nubian, Arabic, and Turkish.[49]

Universities

While the standards for what qualifies as an early university are contested, a good argument can be made that the earliest universities in the world did not spring up in Europe, but instead formed in Tunisia (AD 737), Morocco (AD 858), Egypt (AD 970), and Mali (AD 989)—African all. By comparison, the oldest university in Europe was founded in 1088 in Italy.[50]

Religion and Theology

This point should be obvious, and yet unfortunately it is not. Many of the Church Fathers were Africans, at a time when Europe could hardly tell its right hand from the left in theological matters or Christian formation.

Saint Augustine of Hippo, perhaps the most famous Church Father, was of Berber origin, as were Cyprian and Tertullian (Berber refers to a North African ethnicity). Clement, Origen, Athanasius, and Cyril were Egyptians, as were the Desert Fathers. Much later, European artists painted the African Church Fathers with European features and erased the word African from their profiles. That is why some ludicrously claim these men were not Africans but only came from Roman Africa. They most certainly were Africans. Africans played a crucial role in the history of Christianity. Wisdom and virtue flowed northward.

Further, Africa contributed to Hebrew-Jewish history and society. David Adamo of Delta State University, Abraka, Delta State, Nigeria, traces these contributions in his monumental study.[51] He noted that "Africa and Africans have made significant contributions to the religious life and the civilization of the ancient Near East, and particularly ancient Israel,"[52] and that a "significant place [was] given to Africa and Africans in the religion of Israel."[53]

Among other things, Adamo points out that the Queen of Sheba came from Africa, and that Solomon's temple, "one of the most important institutions in Israel, was built and supported with African wood" and "decorated with African gold, silver, and many precious stones" while "spices were brought to Jerusalem."[54]

Other contributions which should not be overlooked include Hezekiah's religious reform, which may have been influenced or brought about because of the African promise of protection and Hezekiah's trust in the African rulers. The promise of help probably gave Hezekiah the courage to revolt against the powerful Assyrians.[55]

Africa Stands Tall

IN SUMMARY, whether in science or the arts, manufacturing, medical cures, inventions, Christian leadership, architecture, mathematics, astronomy—and the list could go on—African history is radically different from Frederick Lugard's description of it as producing nothing but rudimentary drawings. African history is rich. African contributions are important. Africa has nothing to be ashamed of—rather, let those who sought and seek to demean Africa and the African on the basis of pseudo-scientific Social Darwinism be ashamed.

Africa and Africans are in all ways equal to other ethnicities and nationalities. For we are in the most crucial regards alike. There is only one human race, made up of human beings who are not naturally divided into economic, social, or other spurious classes by birth. As Antonio Rosa puts it, "We are not royals or commoners, slaves, barbarians, savages, capitalists or workers; our primary identity is *humans*."[56]

CONCLUSION:
TWO VIEWS OF HUMANITY

A S WE CONCLUDE, LET US NOW CONSIDER THE TWO VIEWS OF HU-
manity between which each of us must choose. As we have seen,
Darwin and his followers embraced a view of human life as conflict, as
a battle for ascendency, as a fight to the death. It is a view of divisiveness
and discord.

But this view is not the only one. Shortly after the Russian transla-
tion of *The Origin of Species* was published, Nicholas Nozhin, a Russian
scientist, objected to the idea of struggle for life which Darwin insisted
upon. As James Allen Rogers explains, according to Nozhin,

> Darwin talks about the connection between the struggle for existence
> and natural selection as if he did not notice that every such connection
> is limited by the antagonism between these two conditions of growth;
> therefore, he does not see that the struggle for existence is not help-
> ful for development, that by itself it is only the source of pathological
> phenomena, phenomena diametrically opposed to the laws of physical
> development.[1]

Nozhin goes further to clarify his foregoing assertion by citing
what he calls a physiological law which, in his view, renders impossible
any apotheosis of the struggle for existence. In his words, "Identical organisms do not struggle against one another for existence, but on the
contrary, strive to combine one with the other, as it were, to unify their
homogeneous forces, their interests, and by this process, cooperation
rather than a division of labor is observed in their relations."[2]

Many other scientists agree with Nozhin. Indeed, Ashley Montagu has noted that notable biologists such as S. J. Holmes, Patrick Geddes, J. Arthur Thompson, George Gaylord Simpson, Theodosius Dobzhansky, Marston Bates, Warder C. Allee, William Patten, John Muirhead Macfarlane, Ralph Lillie, and Herman J. Muller have all validated Nozhin's position[3] to the effect that "co-operative forces are biologically more important and vital than struggle for survival."[4]

What is of interest herein is the fact that Darwin looked at a phenomenon and saw a struggle to the death, while other scientists saw cooperation for life. These are competing views of reality. On the one hand, there is Darwin's theory, which sees in humans the ongoing struggle for existence, where might makes right. On the other hand, there is a cooperative view best epitomized by a little-known historical occurrence.

It was the night of December 24, 1914, when World War I was raging. The location was a number of points along the six hundred miles of triple trenches that stretched across Belgium and France.[5] The astonishing event began when some German soldiers started singing their Christmas hymn "Stille Nacht" to console themselves for the pittance that their government sent them for Christmas. Soon the British and the French, on the other side of the battle line, joined in with their versions of "Silent Night."

It did not stop there. Soldiers on both sides courageously dropped their weapons and met in the neutral zone, in peace, to speak with their former foes face to face. To get to the neutral zone, they had to climb over barbed wire, walk around shell holes and over frozen corpses (which were later to be given respectful burials during an extension of the truce, with soldiers from both sides helping one another with the gruesome task of burying their comrades). These spontaneous friends "shared chocolate bars, cigarettes, wine, schnapps, soccer games and pictures from home. Addresses were exchanged, [and] photos were taken."[6]

On that night common humanity triumphed over the orders the soldiers had received, over their personal fears and prejudices, over their separate loyalties. The cooperative view of humanity triumphed over the Darwinian fight for existence.

For war and the warlike this posed a problem. Thus this "unplanned-for and unauthorized cease-fire, orchestrated by non-officers and unheard of in the history of warfare... was to become censored out of mainstream history books for most of the next century."

Indeed, "the event was regarded by the professional military officer class to be so profound and so important (and so disturbing) that strategies were immediately put in place that would ensure that such an event could never happen again."[7]

But rest assured, such a thing is like an eclipse; it will happen again.

For this is the truth about humanity. We are children of the Transcendent. We are more than random mutation and natural selection, more than atoms bumping aimlessly in the void, more than mindless forces struggling to survive.

Accepting this reality, and not the warped view of Darwin and his followers, is what will enable Nigeria—and indeed, all the world—to rise and prosper.

ACKNOWLEDGMENTS

First and foremost, I doff my hat to all the excellent people who constituted a link at some point or the other in the chain of events and contributions which resulted in this book, but whose names are not listed one by one in this acknowledgment register, for reasons of space. You all are special. Please take it that this is your book.

I must register my appreciation, first, to the Discovery Institute, for my sponsorship to the United Kingdom in 2018 and 2019 respectively, to enable me to consult in libraries and archives at the University of Edinburgh twice, National Library of Scotland, British National Archive, and the Weston Library at Oxford University. The Institute also funded my research trips locally to the National Archive, Kaduna, and to the branch at Ibadan.

In all of the above, I must highlight the role of Dr. John West, Managing Director of the Discovery Institute's Center for Science and Culture, for his cooperation and for the trust he reposed in me as communication developed between us. Not once did he resort to perfunctory and clinical correspondence; rather, his emails brimmed with trust and encouragement, which at my end also translated increasingly into friendship. John is a great soul.

Thanks also go to Dr. Brian Miller, Research Coordinator at the Center for Science and Culture, Discovery Institute, who helped greatly regarding my understanding of the human eye.

Professor David Ferguson, formerly Professor of Divinity, University of Edinburgh, has always been inspiring since my one-year study at

New College, Edinburgh. He facilitated my research visits in 2018 and 2019 respectively to Edinburgh.

I discovered that it takes just a few minutes of meeting Professor Brian Stanley, Director of the Centre for the Study of World Christianity (CSWC), University of Edinburgh, for one to be abreast of the latest resources in one's area of research.

I have always felt at home at the National Library of Scotland, Edinburgh. On my last visit, it was a privilege to be served by Lorna Black and by Liz MacDonald, General Reading Room Manager, who delivered materials to me with a smile.

It was an honor to be served by the staff and volunteers at SIM archive in South Carolina, especially Evelyn Bowers.

Greatest thanks also to Dr. Tim Gysbeek, Eric Welbourne, Mrs. Joanah Bogunjoko, Martha Bradley, Mrs. Lamikanra, and Kian Flynn for their various most kind help. Dr. Mojisola Kunle Dare graciously took it upon herself to help me with materials that were beyond my reach. I call her *Aburo*; and she calls me *Egbọn*. Londa Schiebinger kindly sent me a digital copy of her book, which was just off the press, *Secret Cures of Slaves: People, Plants, and Medicine in the Eighteenth-Century Atlantic*. Professor Shobana Shankar helpfully forwarded to me several documents, including a digital copy of her book, *Who Shall Enter Paradise?* Dr. Olatunde Oduwobi kindly sent me digital documents as well.

And I must mention retired Most Rev. M. Kehinde Stephen, who would climb a ladder to find anything that might be helpful.

Pastor Jerry Yisa Abraham and Mrs. Deaconess Lydia Abraham, and Dr. (Mrs.) Patricia Olugbemi made sure I had a stopover in Abuja on my way to and from north. The proprietor of Ajoy Hotel, Abuja, provided me with free and comfortable accommodation. Pastor Bamidele Ikumapayi assigned himself the role of unofficial driver, picking me up at different times and in different places, at personal cost, and without complaint even once.

The assistance the staff at the National Museum Library, Onikan, Lagos, rendered is unquantifiable. They include Taiye Pedro, Elizabeth

Abah, Adenike Ipaye, Rukayat Lawani, and Omowunmi Adesuyi. Their work ethic is beyond the bounds of duty. For example, in the onslaught of power outages, which is no news in Nigeria, they would resort to the use of their cell phone accessories to check shelves for materials rather than saying the familiar "there is no light." Furthermore, they salvaged journals beaten by rain from a leaking roof and from underground during the rainy season.

The staff at the National Archive, Kaduna, likewise did a terrific job under conditions not comparable to similar institutions in countries where archival materials are valued as national resources. While all the staff are deserving of recognition, I pay special tribute to Mr. Eke-Nkemka Nnanna and Mike Vonyiri.

And of course I must thank Mrs. Mary Abashiya and Daniel Nuhu Kasai for their kind and gracious help.

Finally and most importantly, I thank God for the roles my wife, Grace, and my children, Isaac Oluseyi, Tolulope Ann, Becky Titilope, and Oluwasanmi Emmanuel played while I was researching and writing this book. I came to realize increasingly the multidimensional display, enablement, and sufficiency of God's grace. Special appreciation to each one of you.

ABOUT THE AUTHOR

Rev. Dr. Olufemi Olayinka Oluniyi (1948–2021) was Executive Director of the Centre for Values and Social Change in Lagos, Nigeria, which he founded. Author of *Reconciliation in Northern Nigeria: The Space for Public Apology*, he was involved in peace, reconciliation, and social justice efforts in Africa for many years, and he had a particular interest in how European colonial policies toward Africa were shaped by Social Darwinism. Dr. Oluniyi was a C.S. Lewis Fellow of Discovery Institute's Center for Science and Culture in the summer of 2017, and he appeared as one of the featured experts in the Institute's award-winning documentary *Human Zoos: America's Forgotten History of Scientific Racism*.

Dr. Oluniyi earned a Master's in Theology from the University of Edinburgh and was a Queen's Cross scholar for his PhD at the University of Aberdeen, which focused on public theology and advocacy journalism. He previously taught at the Niger State College of Education, served as Dean for Academic Affairs for West Africa Theological Seminary, and served as Editorial Board Chair for the National Mirror Newspapers in Nigeria. He was also invited to be a Visiting Research Professor at the Catholic University of America in Washington, DC, although he was unable to accept the appointment. Dr. Oluniyi served as a minister in several congregations throughout his life, and he was on the staff of the Nigerian ministry of Campus Crusade for Christ International from 1979–1981.

ADDITIONAL RESOURCES

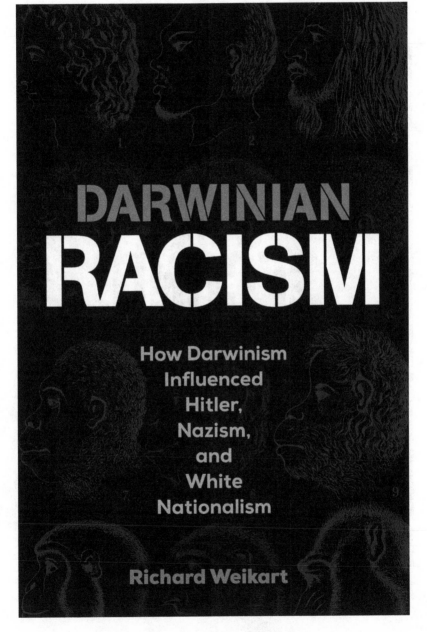

Source: http://www.darwintohitler.com/

Source: http://www.humanzoos.org/

Your Designed Body

Steve Laufmann
Howard Glicksman, MD

Source: http://www.yourdesignedbody.com/

ENDNOTES

PREFACE

1. For various reasons the planned insemination never took place, despite Ivanov's best attempts. This experiment was planned after scientists failed in their attempts to impregnate chimpanzees with human sperm. There have also been other attempts to create a human-monkey embryo. David Albert Jones, "Making Monkeys Out of Us," *Mercatornet*, May 12, 2021, https://mercatornet.com/making-monkeys-out-of-us/71883/. See also "Blasts from the Past: The Soviet Ape-Man Scandal," *New Scientist*, August 20, 2008.

2. See, for instance, Richard Weikart, "Darwinism and Death: Devaluing Human Life in Germany 1859–1920," *Journal of the History of Ideas* 63, no. 2 (April 2002): 323–344.

3. The historian Richard Weikart, for instance, has thoroughly documented the influence of Darwinism on Adolf Hitler and the Nazi party. Clearly and undeniably, Darwinism was used to justify not only the well-known race extermination of the Jews, but also the sterilization or murder of Germans and other "Aryans" deemed "unfit." See Weikart, "Progress through Racial Extermination: Social Darwinism, Eugenics, and Pacifism in Germany, 1860–1918," *German Studies Review* 26, no. 2 (May 2003): 273–294, and Weikart's books, especially *From Darwin to Hilter: Evolutionary Ethics, Eugenics, and Racism in Germany* (New York: Palgrave MacMillan, 2004).

4. For a good (albeit disturbing) overview of the rise of Social Darwinism and the many-faceted worldwide eugenics movement, see the website Eugenics Archive, Social Sciences and Humanities Research Council of Canada, https://eugenicsarchive.ca/.

1. DARWINIAN IMPERIALISM

1. Gregory Claeys, "The 'Survival of the Fittest' and the Origins of Social Darwinism," *Journal of the History of Ideas* 61, no. 2 (April 2000): 227, http://www.jstor.org/stable/3654026. Claeys points out that Darwin, in an 1866 letter, says he wishes he had heard the term sooner, for he "would have worked in 'the survival etc.' often in the new edition of the Origin." Charles Darwin to Alfred Russel Wallace, July 5, 1866, *Darwin Correspondence Project*, Letter no. DCP-LETT-5145, University of Cambridge, https://www.darwinproject.ac.uk/letter/?docId=letters/DCP-LETT-5145.xml.

2. Richard Weikart, "The Origins of Social Darwinism in Germany, 1859–1895," *Journal of the History of Ideas* 54, no. 3 (July 1993): 475, http://www.jstor.org/stable/2710024.

3. Weikart, "The Origins," 476.

4. Rutledge M. Dennis, "Social Darwinism, Scientific Racism, and the Metaphysics of Race," *Journal of Negro Education* 64, no. 3, *Myths and Realities: African Americans and the Measurement of Human Abilities* (Summer 1995): 244, http://www.jstor.org/stable/2967206.

5. See Bernard Lightman, "Darwin and the Popularization of Evolution," *Notes and Records of the Royal Society of London* 64, no. 1 (March 2010), http://www.jstor.org/stable/40647330.

6. Edward J. Larson, "The Rhetoric of Eugenics: Expert Authority and the Mental Deficiency Bill," *British Journal for the History of Science* 24, no. 1 (March 1991), 45–60, http://www.jstor.org/stable/4027015.

7. For an overview of eugenics around the world, see the compilation "Compulsory Sterilization," *International Encyclopedia of the Social and Behavioral Sciences, Science Direct,* https://www.sciencedirect.com/topics/medicine-and-dentistry/compulsory-sterilization.

8. Alberto Specktorowski and Elisabet Mizrachi, "Eugenics and the Welfare State in Sweden: The Politics of Social Margins and the Idea of a Productive Society," *Journal of Contemporary History* 39, no. 3 (July 2004): 333–352, http://www.jstor.org/stable/3180732.

9. John J. Conley, "Margaret Sanger's Extreme Brand of Eugenics," *America: The Jesuit Review,* July 28, 2020, https://www.americamagazine.org/politics-society/2020/07/28/margaret-sangers-extreme-brand-eugenics. See also Dennis, "Social Darwinism, Scientific Racism, and the Metaphysics of Race."

10. Richard Weikart, "Killing the Unfit," Chapter 8 in *From Darwin to Hitler: Evolutionary Ethics, Eugenics and Racism in Germany* (New York: Palgrave MacMillan, 2004).

11. Richard Weikart, "Darwinism and Death: Devaluing Human Life in Germany 1859–1920," *Journal of the History of Ideas* 63, no. 2 (April 2002): 330, https://doi.org/10.2307/3654200.

12. Weikart, "Darwinism and Death," 330.

13. Frank Besag, "Social Darwinism, Race, and Research," *Educational Evaluation and Policy Analysis* 3, no. 1 (January–February 1981): 60, http://www.jstor.org/stable/1163643.

14. Dennis, "Social Darwinism, Scientific Racism, and the Metaphysics of Race," 243. Also see Richard Weikart, *Darwinian Racism: How Darwinism Influenced Hitler, Nazism, and White Nationalism* (Seattle: Discovery Institute Press, 2022), Chapter 1, for more about Darwin's racism.

15. Charles Darwin, *The Descent of Man, and Selection in Relation to Sex,* vol. 1 (London: John Murray, 1871), https://archive.org/details/dli.bengal.10689.8900/page/n3/mode/2up. "Lowest savages" can be seen at 34, 35, 161, 234; "lower races" at 173; and "lowest barbarians" at 34, 64, 94. Darwin also makes frequent references simply to "savages" and "barbarians," including references to "savages" and "barbarians" living during his own time, as at pages 34 and 234.

16. Darwin, *Descent of Man.* References to "highly civilised" and "civilised nations" can be found in many places, including a vast number in Volume 1, Chapter 5.

17. Darwin, *Descent of Man,* 178.

18. Darwin, *Descent of Man,* 160.

19. See Weikart, *From Darwin to Hitler,* esp. 186.

20. Darwin, *Descent of Man,* 201.

21. Darwin, *Descent of Man,* 201, 219. For further documentation see John West, *Darwin Day in American* (Wilmington, DE: ISI Books, 2007), 145–146, 410n145, 410n146.

22. Linneaus used the term "sub species" for animals, but "varieties" for humans, for he believed humans were one species varying in appearance because of geography. See Isabelle

Charmantier, "Linneaus and Race," *Linnean Society of London*, September 3, 2020, https://www.linnean.org/learning/who-was-linnaeus/linnaeus-and-race.

23. Joseph Arthur de Gobineau, *An Essay on the Inequality of the Human Races*. This was originally published as *Essai sur l'inégalité des races humaines* (Paris: Firmin-Didot frères, 1853–1855).

24. Claeys, "The 'Survival of the Fittest,'" 240.

25. Weikart, "The Origins," 477.

26. Weikart "The Origins," 481.

27. Ziegler quoted in Weikart, "The Origins," 481.

28. Weikart, "The Origins," 480. Haeckel later revised the number of species upwards to twelve "and even grouped these species into four separate genera"; see Weikart, "Progress through Racial Extermination: Social Darwinism, Eugenics, and Pacifism in Germany, 1860–1918," *German Studies Review* 26, no. 2 (May 2003): 275.

29. Weikart, "The Origins," 481.

30. Claeys, "The 'Survival of the Fittest,'" 225.

31. Claeys, "The 'Survival of the Fittest,'" 225.

32. Claeys, "The 'Survival of the Fittest,'" 240, 237.

33. Darwin, *Descent of Man*, 162.

34. Claeys, "The 'Survival of the Fittest,'" 225.

35. Weikart, "The Origins," 469.

36. Claeys, "The 'Survival of the Fittest,'" 237.

37. Darwin, *Descent of Man*, 238–239.

38. Darwin, *Descent of Man*, 201.

39. Dennis, "Social Darwinism, Scientific Racism, and the Metaphysics of Race," 245.

2. THE "INFERIOR AFRICAN" NARRATIVE

1. The countries participating were Austria-Hungary, Belgium, Denmark, France, Germany, Great Britain, Italy, the Netherlands, Portugal, Russia, Spain, Sweden-Norway (unified from 1814–1905), Turkey, and the United States of America.

2. See "The Philosophy of Colonialism: Civilization, Christianity, and Commerce," *Violence in Twentieth Century Africa*, Emory University, accessed April 16, 2020, https://scholar-blogs.emory.edu/violenceinafrica/sample-page/the-philosophy-of-colonialism-civilization-christianity-and-commerce/.

3. Lady Lugard, "Nigeria," *Journal of the Society for Arts* 52, no. 2678 (March 18, 1904): 370–384, http://www.jstor.org/stable/41335768.

4. Lady Lugard, "Nigeria," 375.

5. Allen Upward, "The Province of Kabba, Northern Nigeria," *Journal of the Royal African Society* 2, no. 7 (April 1903): 235–260, 257, http://www.jstor.org/stable/715166.

6. Lady Lugard, "The Tropics and the Empire," in *The Empire and the Century*, eds. Charles Sydney Goldman and Rudyard Kipling (London: John Murray, 1905), 821.

7. Lady Lugard, "The Tropics and the Empire," 824.

8. Lady Lugard, "The Tropics and the Empire," 824–825.

9. Flora Lugard, *A Tropical Dependency* (London: James Nisbet and Co., 1906), https://archive.org/details/dli.ernet.16322/page/21/mode/2up.

10. Flora Lugard, *A Tropical Dependency*, 17.

11. I. F. Nicolson, *The Administration of Nigeria, 1900–1960: Men, Methods, and Myths* (Oxford: Clarendon Press, 1969), 171, https://archive.org/details/administrationof0000nico/page/n1/mode/2up.

12. Constance Belcher Larymore, *A Resident's Wife in Nigeria* (London: Routledge and Sons, 1908), https://archive.org/details/residentswifeinn00laryrich/page/n17/mode/2up.

13. Larymore, *A Resident's Wife in Nigeria*, 95.

14. Larymore, *A Resident's Wife in Nigeria*, 95.

15. Larymore, *A Resident's Wife in Nigeria*, 104. This touching event occurred in 1904.

16. Larymore, *A Resident's Wife in Nigeria*, 117–118.

3. British Administrators Echo Darwin

1. Frederick Lugard, "West African Possession and Administration," in *The Empire and the Century*, eds. Charles Sydney Goldman and Rudyard Kipling (London: John Murray, 1905), 859.

2. Lugard, "West African Possession," 860.

3. Walter Russell Crocker, *Nigeria: A Critique of British Colonial Administration* (London: George Allen & Unwin Ltd, 1936), 214, https://archive.org/details/in.ernet.dli.2015.507090.

4. Crocker, *Nigeria: A Critique of British Colonial Administration*, 215.

5. Frederick D. Lugard, *The Dual Mandate in British Tropical Africa* (London: William Blackwood and Sons, 1922), 38, https://archive.org/details/in.ernet.dli.2015.20995.

6. Lugard, *Dual Mandate*, 16.

7. I. F. Nicolson, *The Administration of Nigeria, 1900–1960: Men, Methods, and Myths* (Oxford: Clarendon Press, 1969), 7, https://archive.org/details/administrationof0000nico/page/n1/mode/2up.

8. Lugard, *Dual Mandate*, 197.

9. Lugard, *Dual Mandate*, 36.

10. Lugard, *Dual Mandate*, 72.

11. Lugard, *Dual Mandate*, 67.

12. Lugard, *Dual Mandate*, 67–68.

13. Lugard, *Dual Mandate*, 68–69.

14. Charles Eliot, *The East Africa Protectorate* (London: Arnold, 1905), 92, https://archive.org/details/eastafricaprotec00eliouoft.

15. Eliot, *The East Africa Protectorate*, 92.

16. Lugard, *Dual Mandate*, 70.

17. Karl Pearson, *National Life from the Standpoint of Science* (London: Adam and Charles Black, 1905), 63, https://archive.org/details/nationallifefrom00pearrich.

18. Pearson, *National Life from the Standpoint of Science*, 46.

19. Pearson, *National Life from the Standpoint of Science*, 46.

20. Pearson, *National Life from the Standpoint of Science*, 64.

21. Lugard, *Dual Mandate*, 10.

22. "Benjamin Kidd (1858–1916)," *Clare County Library,* accessed July 28, 2018, http://www. clarelibrary.ie/eolas/coclare/people/benjamin_kidd.htm.

23. Agner Fog, *Cultural Selection* (Boston: Kluwer Academic Publishers, 1999), 21; D. P. Crook, "Kidd, Benjamin (1858–1916)," in *Oxford Dictionary of National Biography,* eds. H. C. G. Matthew and B. Harrison (Oxford: Oxford University Press, 2004).

24. Lugard, *Dual Mandate,* 198.

25. Lugard, *Dual Mandate,* 507.

26. Frederick Lugard, *Annual Colonial Report no. 346, Northern Nigeria, 1900–01* (London: Darling and Son, 1902), https://libsysdigi.library.illinois.edu/ilharvest/Africana/Boo ks2011-05/3064634/3064634_1900_1901_northern_nigeria/3064634_1900_1901_ northern_nigeria_opt.pdf.

27. Frederick Lugard, *Annual Colonial Report no. 409, Northern Nigeria, 1902* (London: Darling and Son, 1903), https://libsysdigi.library.illinois.edu/ilharvest/Africana/Boo ks2011-05/3064634/3064634_1902_northern_nigeria/3064634_1902_northern_nige- ria_opt.pdf.

28. Frederick Lugard, *Annual Colonial Report no. 437, Northern Nigeria, 1903* (London: Darling and Son, 1904), https://libsysdigi.library.illinois.edu/ilharvest/Africana/Boo ks2011-05/3064634/3064634_1903_northern_nigeria/3064634_1903_northern_nige- ria_opt.pdf.

29. Frederick Lugard, *Annual Colonial Report no. 476, Northern Nigeria, 1904* (London: Darling and Son, 1905), https://libsysdigi.library.illinois.edu/ilharvest/Africana/Boo ks2011-05/3064634/3064634_1904_northern_nigeria/3064634_1904_northern_nige- ria_opt.pdf.

30. Charles Temple, *Native Races and Their Rulers: Sketches and Studies of Official Life and Administrative Problems in Nigeria* (London: Way and Co., 1918), vi, https://archive.org/ details/nativeracestheir00tempuoft.

31. Temple, *Native Races,* 21.

32. Temple, *Native Races,* 31.

33. Temple, *Native Races,* 32.

34. Temple, *Native Races,* 21.

35. Temple, *Native Races,* 21.

36. Temple, *Native Races,* 22–23.

37. Temple, *Native Races,* 54.

38. Christopher Alderman, "British Imperialism and Social Darwinism: C. L. Temple and Colonial Administration in Northern Nigeria, 1901–1916," (PhD thesis, Kingston University, 1996), 2–3.

39. Shobana Shankar, *Who Shall Enter Paradise: Christian Origins in Muslim Northern Nigeria, ca. 1890–1975,* New African History Series (Athens, OH: Ohio University Press, 2014), 49. Intermarriage is an idea that Charles Temple could not even contemplate, as he was so horrified to find the French intermarrying so freely with supposedly inferior Arabs on his ill-fated journey from South Africa to England.

40. Robert Heussler, *The British in Northern Nigeria* (London: Oxford University Press, 1968), 124.

41. Heussler, *The British in Northern Nigeria,* 124.

42. Heussler, *The British in Northern Nigeria,* 124.

43. Heussler, *The British in Northern Nigeria*, 125.

44. Heussler, *The British in Northern Nigeria*, 125.

45. Heussler, *The British in Northern Nigeria*, 125.

46. Heussler, *The British in Northern Nigeria*, 123–127. The point of no return referred to a gate or door in the departure halls where slaves bound for the Americas were kept awaiting boarding to their respective ships. As soon as they went through that gate, they were technically out of Africa, and were counted as belonging to their respective destinations.

47. Nicolson, *The Administration of Nigeria*, 107.

48. William MacGregor, "Lagos, Abeokuta and the Alake," *Journal of the Royal African Society* 3, no. 12 (July 1904), 466, http://www.jstor.org/stable/715226.

49. MacGregor, "Lagos, Abeokuta and the Alake."

4. THE EVOLUTIONARY LADDER

1. Margery Perham, "Some Problems of Indirect Rule in Africa," *Journal of the Royal African Society* 34, no. 135 (April 1935): 4, http://www.jstor.org/stable/717145.

2. Erik Gilbert and Jonathan T. Reynolds, *Africa in World History: From Prehistory to the Present*, 2nd ed. (Upper Saddle River: Pearson, 2008), 327.

3. C. Gordon Beacham, *New Frontiers in the Central Sudan* (Toronto: Evangelical Publishers, 1928), 30.

4. Albert David Helser, *In Sunny Nigeria: Experiences Among a Primitive People in the Interior of North Central Africa* (New York: Fleming H. Revell Company, 1926), 102n2; 139.

5. Walter Richard Samuel Miller, *Reflections of a Pioneer* (London: Church Missionary Society, 1936), 53.

6. Walter Miller, *Success in Nigeria? Assets and Possibilities* (London: Lutterworth Press, 1948), 77.

7. Chinedu Ubah, "The Sokoto Caliphate: The Ideals of 1804 and the Realities of 2004," in *The Sokoto Caliphate: History and Legacies, 1804–2004*, vol. 2 (Kaduna: Arewa House, 2006), 357.

8. Frederick Lugard, *Annual Colonial Report no. 409, Northern Nigeria, 1902* (London: Darling and Son, 1903), 19, https://libsysdigi.library.illinois.edu/ilharvest/Africana/Boo ks2011-05/3064634/3064634_1902_northern_nigeria/3064634_1902_northern_nige-ria_opt.pdf.

9. Frederick Lugard, *Annual Colonial Report no. 437, Northern Nigeria, 1903* (London: Darling and Son, 1904), 4, https://libsysdigi.library.illinois.edu/ilharvest/Africana/Boo ks2011-05/3064634/3064634_1903_northern_nigeria/3064634_1903_northern_nige-ria_opt.pdf.

10. Lugard, *Annual Colonial Report no. 409*, 28.

11. Lugard, *Annual Colonial Report no. 409*, 62.

12. Frederick D. Lugard, *The Dual Mandate in British Tropical Africa* (London: William Blackwood and Sons, 1922), 67–68, https://archive.org/details/in.ernet.dli.2015.20995.

13. Frederick Lugard, *Annual Colonial Report no. 346, Northern Nigeria, 1900–01* (London: Darling and Son, 1902), 15, https://libsysdigi.library.illinois.edu/ilharvest/Africana/Bo oks2011-05/3064634/3064634_1900_1901_northern_nigeria/3064634_1900_1901_northern_nigeria_opt.pdf.

14. Lugard, *Dual Mandate*, 198.

15. Lugard, *Dual Mandate*, 210.

16. Lady Lugard, "Nigeria," *Journal of the Society for Arts* 52, no. 2678 (March 18, 1904): 370–384, http://www.jstor.org/stable/41335768.

17. Flora Lugard, *A Tropical Dependency* (London: James Nisbet and Co., 1906), 22, https://archive.org/details/dli.ernet.16322/page/21/mode/2up.

18. Flora Lugard, *A Tropical Dependency*, 158.

19. Lady Lugard, "Nigeria," 374.

20. Flora Lugard, *A Tropical Dependency*, 375.

21. Qtd in I. F. Nicolson, *The Administration of Nigeria, 1900–1960: Men, Methods, and Myths* (Oxford: Clarendon Press, 1969), 168, https://archive.org/details/administrationof-0000nico/page/n1/mode/2up.

22. Lady Lugard, "Nigeria," 372.

23. Nicolson, *The Administration of Nigeria*, 108.

24. Nicolson, *The Administration of Nigeria*, 107.

25. Charles William James Orr, *The Making of Northern Nigeria* (London: Macmillan & Co., 1911), 67https://archive.org/details/makingofnorthern0000orrc.

26. Christopher Alderman, "British Imperialism and Social Darwinism: C. L. Temple and colonial administration in Northern Nigeria, 1901–1916" (PhD thesis, Kingston University, 1996); Charles Lindsay Temple, "Northern Nigeria," *The Geographical Journal* 40, no. 2 (August 1912): 149, http://www.jstor.org/stable/1778461.

27. Temple, "Northern Nigeria."

28. Temple, "Northern Nigeria," 153.

29. Charles Temple, *Native Races and Their Rulers: Sketches and Studies of Official Life and Administrative Problems in Nigeria* (London: Way and Co., 1918), 22–23, https://archive.org/details/nativeracestheir00tempuoft.

30. Lugard, *Dual Mandate*, 198.

31. Flora Lugard, *A Tropical Dependency*, 481.

5. ELEVATING ISLAM

1. Frederick D. Lugard, *The Dual Mandate in British Tropical Africa* (London: William Blackwood and Sons, 1922), 67–68, *https://archive.org/details/in.ernet.dli.2015.20995*.

2. Flora Lugard, *A Tropical Dependency* (London: James Nisbet and Co., 1906), 317, https://archive.org/details/dli.ernet.16322/page/21/mode/2up.

3. Frederick Lugard, *Annual Colonial Report no. 476, Northern Nigeria, 1904* (London: Darling and Son, 1905), 47, https://libsysdigi.library.illinois.edu/ilharvest/Africana/Books2011-05/3064634/3064634_1904_northern_nigeria/3064634_1904_northern_nigeria_opt.pdf.

4. Flora Lugard, *A Tropical Dependency*, 21.

5. Lugard, *Dual Mandate*, 76.

6. Lugard, *Dual Mandate*, 210

7. Lugard, *Dual Mandate*, 77.

8. Lugard, *Dual Mandate*, 78.

9. Walter Russell Crocker, *Nigeria: A Critique of British Colonial Administration* (London: George Allen & Unwin Ltd, 1936), 223, https://archive.org/details/in.ernet.dli.2015.507090.

10. Lugard, *Dual Mandate*, 78.

11. Lugard, *Dual Mandate*, 77.

12. Crocker, *Nigeria: A Critique of British Colonial Administration*, 224.

13. Crocker, *Nigeria: A Critique of British Colonial Administration*, 226.

14. Crocker, *Nigeria: A Critique of British Colonial Administration*, 225–226.

15. Crocker, *Nigeria: A Critique of British Colonial Administration*, 225.

16. Edmund Dene Morel, *Nigeria: Its Peoples and Its Problems* [1911] (London: Thomas Nelson, 1968), 219.

17. Crocker, *Nigeria: A Critique of British Colonial Administration*, 226–227.

18. Lugard, *Dual Mandate*, 78.

19. Lugard, *Dual Mandate*, 594.

6. Anti-Darwinian Christians

1. Erik Gilbert and Jonathan T. Reynolds, *Africa in World History: From Prehistory to the Present*, 2nd ed. (Upper Saddle River: Pearson, 2008), 328.

2. E. A. Ayandele, "The Missionary Factor in Northern Nigeria, 1870–1918," *Journal of the Historical Society of Nigeria* 3, no. 3 (December 1966): 517.

3. Sonia Graham, *Government and Mission Education in Northern Nigeria 1900–1919* (Ibadan: Ibadan University Press, 1966). Graham describes in great and careful detail the interactions between missionaries and administrators in Northern Nigeria as missionaries sought to establish schools without causing conflict.

4. Walter Richard Samuel Miller, *Reflections of a Pioneer* (London: Church Missionary Society, 1936), 92.

5. Gilbert and Reynolds, *Africa in World History*, 328.

6. The correspondence surrounding this matter is housed in box 12, folder 5, Weston Library, Bodleian Libraries, University of Oxford. There are letters pertaining to the issue between Mr. Hooper (CMS Secretary) and Lugard on June 9, 1936; June 10, 1936; and July 20, 1936. Letters between Lugard and Miller are dated June 24, 1936; June 25, 1936; July 20, 1936; and July 22, 1936.

7. Herbert Symons Goldsmith, "Administrative Policy in Northern Nigeria," *West African Review* (January 1937): 11–13. E. J. Arnett, "I Disagree with Dr. Miller," *West African Review* (February 1937): 16–18.

8. C. Morgan, "Independent Testimony" in *Lightbearer*, Sudan United Mission, November 1907, 239.

9. Miller, *Reflections of a Pioneer*, 88.

10. Walter Miller, *Have We Failed in Nigeria?* (London: Lutterworth Press, 1947), 24.

11. Thomas Jefferson Bowen, *Adventures in Missionary Labours in Several Countries in the Interior of Africa from 1849 to 1856* [1857] (London: Frank Cass & Co., 1968), 284.

12. Bowen, *Adventures in Missionary Labours*, 287. For more on Yoruba bargaining practices in the village square ancient and modern, see Olufemi Olayinka Oluniyi, *Reconciliation in Northern Nigeria* (Lagos, Nigeria: Frontier Press, 2017), 102–103.

13. Bowen, *Adventures in Missionary Labours*, 280–281.

14. Bowen, *Adventures in Missionary Labours*, 281.

15. Bowen, *Adventures in Missionary Labours*, 280.

16. Bowen, *Adventures in Missionary Labours*, 284.

17. Bowen, *Adventures in Missionary Labours*, 288.

18. Summer Institute of Linguistics (SIL) Nigeria, Jos, Plateau State, Nigeria. Information on Christian figures is accurate as of March 2019.

19. Graham, *Government and Mission Education in Northern Nigeria*, 22. Graham's original source is CMS publication no. 88, a letter between Bennet and Gravesend, July 2, 1900.

20. Ethel Neale Thamer, *Little Is Much When God Is in It* (self-published, ca. 1991), 47.

21. Niels Kastfelt, *Religion and Politics in Nigeria: A Study in Middle Belt Christianity* (London: British Academic Press, 1994), 57.

22. Matthew 28:19–20, Mark 16:15.

23. J. B. Webster, "The Bible and the Plough," *Journal of the Historical Society of Nigeria* 2, no. 4 (December 1963), http://www.jstor.org/stable/41856670.

24. S. S. Berry, "Christianity and the Rise of Cocoa-Growing in Ibadan and Ondo," *Journal of the Historical Society of Nigeria* 4, no. 3 (December 1968), 439–451, http://www.jstor.org/stable/41856765.

25. J. Ade Ajayi, *Christian Missions in Nigeria 1841–1891: The Making of a New Elite* (Evaston: Northwestern University Press, 1964), 91.

26. Conversation with Pa Modupe Oduyoye, former Literature Secretary of the Christian Council of Nigeria and Manager, Daystar Press, Ibadan.

27. Shobana Shankar, *Who Shall Enter Paradise: Christian Origins in Muslim Northern Nigeria, ca. 1890–1975*, New African History Series (Athens, OH: Ohio University Press, 2014), 78.

28. Ajayi, *Christian Missions*, 15.

29. Ajayi, *Christian Missions*, 85, 14.

30. Ajayi, *Christian Missions*, 91.

31. Ajayi, *Christian Missions*, 147.

32. Ajayi, *Christian Missions*, 156.

33. Ajayi, *Christian Missions*, 157.

34. Ajayi, *Christian Missions*, 146.

35. Ajayi, *Christian Missions*, 156

36. Nimishillen Old German Baptist Brethren Church, Ohio, 937; I received this two-page digitized attachment from the Brethren archive, but with incomplete bibliographic information.

37. Ajayi, *Christian Missions*, 158.

38. Ajayi, *Christian Missions*, 159.

39. Ajayi, *Christian Missions*, 159.

40. Ajayi, *Christian Missions*, 160.

41. Ajayi, *Christian Missions*, 159, 160.

42. Walter Miller, "Ought Christian Missions to be Allowed in Moslem Lands?," *Lightbearer*, Sudan United Mission, 1912, 53.

43. Ayandele, "The Missionary Factor in Northern Nigeria," 505–507.

44. See Walter Miller, *Walter Miller, 1872–1952: An Autobiography* (Zaria, Nigeria: Gaskiya Corporation, 1953), 31.

45. Margery Perham, *Lugard: The Years of Authority, 1898-1945*, vol. 2 (London: Collins, 1960), 494–495, https://archive.org/details/lugardyearsofaut0000unse.

46. Graham, *Government and Mission Education in Northern Nigeria*, 132.

47. Charles Temple, *Native Races and Their Rulers: Sketches and Studies of Official Life and Administrative Problems in Nigeria* (London: Way and Co., 1918), 212, https://archive.org/details/nativeracestheir00tempuoft.

48. Temple, *Native Races*, 212.

49. Ayandele, "The Missionary Factor in Northern Nigeria," 516.

50. Ayandele, "The Missionary Factor in Northern Nigeria," 516.

51. Jan Harm Boer, *Missionary Messengers of Liberation in a Colonial Context: A Case Study of the Sudan United Mission* (Amsterdam: Rodopi, 1979), 159.

52. Temple, *Natives Races*, 213–214.

53. Temple, *Native Races*, 216.

54. Boer, *Missionary Messengers*, 160.

55. Graham describes one such relocation, that of the CMS mission at Bida, in *Government and Mission Education in Northern Nigeria*, 161.

56. Miller, "Ought Christian Missions to be Allowed in Moslem Lands?," 50–52.

7. EDUCATION: KEEPING THE DARK MAN IN THE DARK

1. Chimamanda Ngozi Adichie, "Things Left Unsaid," *London Review of Books* 34, no. 19 (October 11, 2012), https://www.lrb.co.uk/the-paper/v34/n19/chimamanda-adichie/things-left-unsaid.

2. E. A. Ayandele, "The Missionary Factor in Northern Nigeria, 1870–1918," *Journal of the Historical Society of Nigeria* 3, no. 3 (December 1966): 518.

3. Ayandele, "The Missionary Factor in Northern Nigeria," 518.

4. Ayandele, "The Missionary Factor in Northern Nigeria," 518.

5. I. F. Nicolson, *The Administration of Nigeria, 1900–1960: Men, Methods, and Myths* (Oxford: Clarendon Press, 1969), 139, 137, https://archive.org/details/administrationof0000nico/page/n1/mode/2up.

6. Charles Temple, *Native Races and Their Rulers: Sketches and Studies of Official Life and Administrative Problems in Nigeria* (London: Way and Co., 1918), 219, https://archive.org/details/nativeracestheir00tempuoft.

7. Temple, *Native Races*, 221.

8. Walter Miller, *Walter Miller, 1872–1952: An Autobiography* (Zaria, Nigeria: Gaskiya Corporation, 1953), 28.

9. Sonia Graham, *Government and Mission Education in Northern Nigeria 1900–1919* (Ibadan, Nigeria: Ibadan University Press, 1966), 8, 19, 22.

10. Frederick D. Lugard, *The Dual Mandate in British Tropical Africa* (London: William Blackwood and Sons, 1922), 454, https://archive.org/details/in.ernet.dli.2015.20995.

11. Lugard, *Dual Mandate*, 453.

12. A. Ogunsola, "An Historical Study of the Impact of Education Ordinances on Education in Northern Nigeria, 1916–1966" (PhD diss., Ohio University, 1970), 17.

13. Lugard, *Dual Mandate*, 454n1.

14. Graham, *Government and Mission Education in Northern Nigeria*, 24.

15. Graham, *Government and Mission Education in Northern Nigeria*, 29–30.

16. Graham, *Government and Mission Education in Northern Nigeria*, 40.

17. Graham, *Government and Mission Education in Northern Nigeria*, 45–54.

18. Margery Perham, *Lugard: The Years of Authority, 1898-1945*, vol. 2 (London: Collins, 1960), 495, https://archive.org/details/lugardyearsofaut0000unse.

19. Graham, *Government and Mission Education in Northern Nigeria*, 33–34.

20. Graham, *Government and Mission Education in Northern Nigeria*, 57.

21. Vischer was proficient in Hausa and Kanuri.

22. Graham, *Government and Mission Education in Northern Nigeria*, 74–75.

23. Article 13e of the Education Ordinance 1916, cited in Ogunsola, "An Historical Study," 48.

24. Ogunsola, "An Historical Study," 50; Graham, *Government and Mission Education in Northern Nigeria*, 144–145.

25. Graham, *Government and Mission Education in Northern Nigeria*, 164.

26. Ogunsola, "An Historical Study," 52.

27. Alexander Fraser, *Report on Nigerian Tour: Northern Nigeria*, 1927, 11.

28. Fraser, *Report on Nigerian Tour*, 5.

29. Fraser, *Report on Nigerian Tour*, 11.

30. Fraser, *Report on Nigerian Tour*, 6.

31. Fraser, *Report on Nigerian Tour*, 7.

32. Oldham was a member of the committee to which Fraser submitted his report. He also was Fraser's brother-in-law.

33. Alexander Fraser, foreword to Walter Miller, *Have We Failed in Nigeria?* (London: Lutterworth Press, 1947), 10.

34. Quoted in R. Bunting, *The Educated African* (New York: Fredrick A. Praeger, 1962), 365. Cited in Ogunsola, "An Historical Study," 53.

35. Miller, *Have We Failed in Nigeria?*, 82–83.

36. Walter Richard Samuel Miller, *Reflections of a Pioneer* (London: Church Missionary Society, 1936), 190.

37. Walter Miller, "The Future of the Sudan," *Look on the Field*, 1909, 62–63; *Lightbearer*, Sudan United Mission, August 1909, 154, Miller's list.

38. Ross Jones, "Borgu History," accessed on August 9, 2011. Unfortunately this website appears to have been decommissioned.

39. Frederick Lugard, *Annual Colonial Report no. 409, Northern Nigeria, 1902* (London: Darling and Son, 1903), 14, https://libsysdigi.library.illinois.edu/ilharvest/Africana/Books2011-05/3064634/3064634_1902_northern_nigeria/3064634_1902_northern_nigeria_opt.pdf.

40. Walter Russell Crocker, *Nigeria: A Critique of British Colonial Administration* (London: George Allen & Unwin Ltd, 1936), 215, https://archive.org/details/in.ernet.dli.2015.507090.

41. Jan Harm Boer, *Missionary Messengers of Liberation in a Colonial Context: A Case Study of the Sudan United Mission* (Amsterdam: Rodopi, 1979), 193.

42. Boer, *Missionary Messengers*, 212.

43. *Lightbearer,* Sudan United Mission, March 1934, 26; cited in Boer, *Missionary Messengers,* 272–273.

8. Darwinian Legacy

1. Wale Oyemakinde, "Railway Construction and Operation in Nigeria, 1895–1911: Labour Problems and Socio-Economic Impact," *Journal of the Historical Society of Nigeria* 7, no. 2 (June 1974), 303–324, https://www.jstor.org/stable/41857015; Wale Oyemakinde, "The Role of Government in the Promotion of Agriculture," *An Economic History of West Africa Since 1750*, eds. G. Ogunremii and E. Faluyi (Ibadan: CCCRex Charles Publication, 1996), 189–198.

2. I. F. Nicolson, *The Administration of Nigeria, 1900–1960: Men, Methods, and Myths* (Oxford: Clarendon Press, 1969), 133, https://archive.org/details/administrationof0000nico/page/n1/mode/2up.

3. Nicolson, *The Administration of Nigeria*, 135.

4. Lugard, *Annual Report 1906*. Quoted in Nicolson, *The Administration of Nigeria*, 135.

5. Margery Perham, *Lugard: The Years of Authority, 1898-1945*, vol. 2 (London: Collins, 1960), 171, https://archive.org/details/lugardyearsofaut0000unse. Quoted in Nicolson, *The Administration of Nigeria*, 133.

6. Perham, *The Years of Authority*, 296.

7. Nicolson, *The Administration of Nigeria*, 134.

8. Walter Miller, *Yesterday and Tomorrow in Northern Nigeria* (London: Student Christian Movement Press, 1938), 34.

9. Both railway development and the blocking of land ownership primarily took place under High Commissioner Percy Girouard, who governed Northern Nigeria from 1907–1912, during Lugard's absence.

10. William Geary, *Nigeria under British Rule* [1927] (New York: Barnes & Noble, 1965), 238, https://archive.org/details/nigeriaunderbrit0000gear.

11. Geary, *Nigeria under British Rule*, 239–240. See also William Geary, "Land Tenure and Legislation in British West Africa," *Journal of the Royal African Society* 12, no. 47 (April 1913): 244, http://www.jstor.org/stable/715884.

12. Perham, *The Years of Authority*, 171.

13. Nicolson, *The Administration of Nigeria*, 304.

14. Nicolson, *The Administration of Nigeria*, 149.

15. Nicolson, *The Administration of Nigeria*, 171.

16. Nicolson, *The Administration of Nigeria*, 125.

17. Nicolson, *The Administration of Nigeria*, 126.

18. Nicolson, *The Administration of Nigeria*, 305.

19. Ashley Montagu, *Darwin, Competition, and Cooperation* (New York: Henry Schuman, 1952), 96. Quoted in George E. Simpson, "Darwin and 'Social Darwinism,'" *Antioch Review* 19, no. 1, *The Origin of Species, 100 Years Later* (Spring 1959): 38, http://www.jstor.org/stable/4610123.

20. Isaac Madubuogo Okonjo, *British Administration in Nigeria 1900–1950: A Nigerian View* (New York: Nok Publishers, 1974), 38–40.

21. A. Ogunsola, "An Historical Study of the Impact of Education Ordinances on Education in Northern Nigeria, 1916–1966" (PhD diss., Ohio University, 1970), 112; see also Walter Miller, *Have We Failed in Nigeria?* (London: Lutterworth Press, 1947), 82–83.

22. Terry McGovern, Monique Baumont, and Samantha Garbers, "Customary and Religious Laws are Impeding Progress Towards Women's Health in Nigeria," *Conversation*, February 11, 2021, https://theconversation.com/customary-and-religious-laws-are-impeding-progress-towards-womens-health-in-nigeria-154221.

23. Olufemi Oluniyi, *Reconciliation in Northern Nigeria: The Space for Public Apology* (Lagos, Nigeria: Frontier Press, 2017), xxii.

24. Oluniyi, *Reconciliation in Northern Nigeria*, xxvi.

25. Oluniyi, *Reconciliation in Northern Nigeria*, xxviii.

9. Could Humans Have Evolved?

1. Charles Darwin, *On the Origin of Species by Means of Natural Selection, or the Preservation of Favoured Races in the Struggle for Life* (London: John Murray, 1859), 149.

2. Darwin, *Origin*, 149; emphasis on the word "if" and the word "then" is mine.

3. Otangelo Grasso, "The Evolution of the Eye, Demystified," *Evolution News and Science Today*, February 24, 2020, https://evolutionnews.org/2020/02/the-evolution-of-the-eye-demystified/.

4. Grasso, "The Evolution of the Eye."

5. Brian Miller, "Eye Evolution: A Closer Look," *Evolution News and Science Today*, February 13, 2017, https://evolutionnews.org/2017/02/eye_evolution_a/.

6. Brian Miller explained this in an email message to me on April 25, 2020.

7. Brian Miller, "Eye Evolution: The Waiting Is the Hardest Part," *Evolution News and Science Today*, February 15, 2017, https://evolutionnews.org/2017/02/eye_evolution_t/.

8. Brian Miller in an email clarification to this author on December 4, 2019.

9. Wolf-Ekkehard Lönnig, "Neo-Darwinism and the Big Bang of Man's Origin," *Evolution News and Science Today*, February 25, 2020, https://evolutionnews.org/2020/02/neo-darwinism-and-the-big-bang-of-mans-origin/.

10. Lönnig, "Neo-Darwinism."

11. Bernardo Kastrup, "Consciousness Cannot Have Evolved," *IAI News*, February 5, 2020, https://iai.tv/articles/consciousness-cannot-have-evolved-auid-1302.

10. Are We Just Animals?

1. Jeffrey Schwartz, *Sudden Origins: Fossils, Genes, and the Emergence of Species* (New York: John Wiley and Sons, 1999), 378.

2. Ian Tattersall, *Masters of the Planet: The Search for Our Human Origins* (New York: Palgrave MacMillan, 2012), 207, cited in Wolf-Ekkehard Lönnig, "Neo-Darwinism and the

Big Bang of Man's Origin," *Evolution News and Science Today*, February 25, 2020, https://evolutionnews.org/2020/02/neo-darwinism-and-the-big-bang-of-mans-origin/.

3. Arthur James Balfour, "Theism and Humanism," *Gifford Lectures* (New York: Hodder & Stoughton, 1915).

4. Wesley J. Smith, *A Rat Is a Pig Is a Dog Is a Boy: The Human Cost of the Animal Rights Movement* (New York: Encounter Books, 2010). Some of Smith's earlier works, as far back as 1993, dwell on the same idea, without specifically using that phrase.

5. "Human Exceptionalism," *Wikipedia*, accessed February 6, 2021, https://rationalwiki.org/wiki/Human_exceptionalism.

6. Jonathan Marks, "What is the Viewpoint of Haemoglobin, and Does It Matter?," *History and the Philosophy of the Life Sciences* 31, no. 2 (2009): 246.

7. Ann Gauger, "On Being Human—A Reflection," *Evolution News and Science Today*, January 10, 2019, https://evolutionnews.org/2019/01/on-being-human-a-reflection/.

8. Gauger, "On Being Human."

9. Balfour, "Theism and Humanism," 108–109.

10. John West, "Darwin in the Dock: C. S. Lewis's Critique of Evolution and Evolutionism," in *The Magician's Twin: C. S. Lewis on Science, Scientism and Society*, ed. John West (Seattle: Discovery Institute Press, 2012), 132.

11. Balfour, "Theism and Humanism," 142.

12. C. S. Lewis, "The Funeral of a Great Myth," cited in West, "Darwin in the Dock," 137.

13. Michael Egnor, "Why Pioneer Neurosurgeon Wilder Penfield Said the Mind Is More than the Brain," interview by Robert J. Marks, *Mind Matters News*, February 29, 2020, https://mindmatters.ai/2020/02/why-pioneer-neurosurgeon-wilder-penfield-said-the-mind-is-more-than-the-brain/.

14. Egnor, "Pioneer Neurosurgeon Wilder Penfield."

15. Egnor, "Pioneer Neurosurgeon Wilder Penfield."

16. Egnor, "Pioneer Neurosurgeon Wilder Penfield."

17. Egnor, "Pioneer Neurosurgeon Wilder Penfield."

18. Richard Leblanc, "The White Paper: Wilder Penfield, the Stream of Consciousness, and the Physiology of Mind" *Journal of the History of the Neurosciences* 28, no. 4 (2019): 416–436, https://doi.org/10.1080/0964704X.2019.1651135.

19. See "Wilder Penfield, 1891–1976," in *A Science Odyssey: People and Discoveries*, PBS, 1998, *http://www.pbs.org/wgbh/aso/databank/entries/bhpenf.html*.

20. Parashkev Nachev, "Love: Is It Just a Fleeting High Fuelled by Brain Chemicals," *The Conversation*, February 13, 2020, https://theconversation.com/love-is-it-just-a-fleeting-high-fuelled-by-brain-chemicals-129201.

21. Nachev, "Love."

22. Nachev, "Love."

11. ARE THERE FOUNDATIONAL DIFFERENCES?

1. Peter Wade, Audrey Smedley, and Yasuko I. Takezawa, "Race," *Encyclopedia Britannica*, January 29, 2020, https://www.britannica.com/topic/race-human, available in a more readable form at *Transcend Media Service*, March 23, 2020, https://www.transcend.org/tms/2020/03/race/.

2. Wade, Smedley, and Takezawa, "Race."

3. Wade, Smedley, and Takezawa, "Race."

4. Wade, Smedley, and Takezawa, "Race."

5. "Otto Klineberg," *Wikipedia*, last modified May 7, 2022, https://en.wikipedia.org/wiki/Otto_Klineberg.

6. Rutledge M. Dennis, "Social Darwinism, Scientific Racism, and the Metaphysics of Race," *The Journal of Negro Education*, 64, no. 3, *Myths and Realities: African Americans and the Measurement of Human Abilities* (Summer 1995): 243, http://www.jstor.org/stable/2967206.

7. Koozma J. Tarasoff, "Jena Declaration: The Concept of Race Is the Result of Racism, Not Its Prerequisite," *Transcend Media Service*, March 23, 2020, https://www.transcend.org/tms/2020/03/jena-declaration-the-concept-of-race-is-the-result-of-racism-not-its-prerequisite/.

8. Tarasoff, "Jena Declaration."

9. Walter Miller, *Reflections of a Pioneer* (London: Church Missionary Society, 1936), 195.

10. Genesis 1:27, "So God created mankind in his own image, in the image of God he created them; male and female he created them." New International Version.

11. Bernard Lightman, "Darwin and the Popularization of Evolution," *Notes and Records of the Royal Society of London* 64, no. 1 (March 2010): 8, http://www.jstor.org/stable/40647330.

12. Sharon Kingsland, "Evolution and Debates over Human Progress from Darwin to Sociobiology," *Population and Development Review* 14, Supplement: Population and Resources in Western Intellectual Traditions (1988): 173, http://www.jstor.org/stable/2808095.

13. Richard Weikart, "Darwinism and Death: Devaluing Human Life in Germany 1859-1920," *Journal of the History of Ideas* 63, no. 2 (April 2002): 328–329, https://doi.org/10.2307/3654200.

14. Kingsland, "Evolution and Debates," 185.

15. Weikart, "Darwinism and Death," 328–329.

16. Peter Weingart, Jürgen Kroll, and Kurt Bayertz, *Rasse, Blut, und Gene: Gerschichte der Eugenik und Rassenhygiene in Deutschland* (Frankfurt: Suhrkamp Verlag, 1988), 18. Quoted in Weikart, "Darwinism and Death," 327.

17. Alexander Tille, "Charles Darwin and Ethics," *Die Zukunft* 8 (Berlin, 1894), 302–314, summarized by Weikart, "Darwinism and Death," 327.

18. Then as now, some Christians were willing to entertain Darwin's theory of evolution, attempting in various ways to reconcile it with the scriptural vision of the special creation and exceptional nature of man. See Dennis, "Social Darwinism, Scientific Racism, and the Metaphysics of Race," 245. Some scientists likewise attempted to retain supernatural elements along with Darwin's theory of evolution. See Lightman, "Darwin and the Popularization of Evolution."

12. THE NOT-SO-DARK CONTINENT

1. Christopher Alderman, "British Imperialism and Social Darwinism: C. L. Temple and Colonial Administration in Northern Nigeria, 1901–1916" (PhD thesis, Kingston University, 1996), 107.

2. Olive Temple, *Notes on the Tribes, Provinces, Emirates and States of the Northern Provinces of Nigeria*, 2nd ed. (Lagos: The CMS Bookshop, 1922), 282.

3. *Lightbearer*, March 1907, 63.

4. *Lightbearer*, April 1907, 93.

5. Flora Lugard, *A Tropical Dependency: An Outline of the Ancient History of the Western Soudan with an Account of the Modern Settlement of Northern Nigeria* (London: James Nisbet & Co., 1906), 337.

6. Thomas Bowen, *Adventures and Missionary Labours in Several Countries in the Interior of Africa from 1849–1856*, 2nd ed. (London: Frank Cass, 1968), 286.

7. Alice Gorman, "Australian Archaeologists Dropped the Term 'Stone Age' Decades Ago, and So Should You," *The Conversation*, August 27, 2018, https://theconversation.com/australian-archaeologists-dropped-the-term-stone-age-decades-ago-and-so-should-you-47275.

8. Gorman, "Australian Archaeologists."

9. Frederick D. Lugard, *The Dual Mandate in British Tropical Africa* (London: William Blackwood and Sons, 1922), 1, https://archive.org/details/in.ernet.dli.2015.20995.

10. Lugard, *Dual Mandate*, 66.

11. Sophia "Ankhobia" Carvalho and Clive Harris, "Africa Before the Slave Trade," in *Three Continents, One History: Birmingham, the Transatlantic Slave Trade and the Caribbean*, ed. Clive Harris (Birmingham: Afro-Caribbean Millennium Centre, 2008), 12.

12. Carvalho and Harris, "Africa Before," 13.

13. Carvalho and Harris, "Africa Before," 14.

14. Carvalho and Harris, "Africa Before," 14.

15. Carvalho and Harris, "Africa Before," 16.

16. Carvalho and Harris, "Africa Before," 16.

17. Carvalho and Harris, "Africa Before," 16.

18. See Michael Gomez, *African Dominion: A New History of Empire in Early and Medieval West Africa* (Princeton, NJ: Princeton University Press, 2018), 100.

19. Carvalho and Harris, "Africa Before," 17.

20. Gomez, *African Dominion*, 102. That any Africans reached the Americas in such an early voyage is widely contested, but in addition to Gomez's pro-and-con discussion, see historical documents supporting the view, in Samuel Eliot Morison, translator and editor, *Journals and Other Documents on the Life and Voyages of Christopher Columbus* (New York: Heritage Press, 1963), 262–263.

21. Flora Lugard, *A Tropical Dependency*, 82.

22. Flora Lugard, "West African Negroland," in *Proceedings of the Royal Colonial Institute*, vol. 35, 1903–1904, 318. For more on the subject of gunpowder and firearms in this period and region, see Humphrey J. Fisher and Virginia Rowland, "Firearms in the Central Sudan," *The Journal of African History* 12, no. 2 (April 1971), 215–239.

23. Carvalho and Harris, "Africa Before," 17.

24. Lester Brooks, *Great Civilizations of Ancient Africa* (New York: Four Winds Press, 1971), 7–10.

25. Charles Lindsay Temple, "Northern Nigeria," *The Geographical Journal* 40, no. 2 (August 1912): 161, http://www.jstor.org/stable/1778461.

26. Olive Temple, *Notes on the Tribes, Provinces, Emirates and States of Northern Nigeria* (Lagos: CMS Bookshop), 6.

27. Constance Larymore, *A Resident's Wife in Nigeria* (London: George Routledge & Sons, Ltd, 1908), 30.

28. Charles Henry Robinson, *Nigeria, Our Latest Protectorate* (London: Horace Marshall and Son, 1900), 138.

29. William MacGregor, "Lagos, Abeokuta and the Alake," *Journal of the Royal African Society* 3, no. 12 (July 1904): 478, http://www.jstor.org/stable/715226.

30. Allister Hinds, "Colonial Policy and Nigerian Cotton Exports, 1939-1951," *International Journal of African Historical Studies* 29, no. 1 (1996): 26, http://www.jstor.org/stable/221417.

31. *Lightbearer,* June 1906, 106.

32. Gordon Beacham, *New Frontiers in the Central Sudan* (Toronto: Evangelical Publishers, 1928), 26.

33. Beacham, *New Frontiers in the Central Sudan,* 148.

34. "Ancient Astronomy in Africa," University of Texas, Fall 1998, accessed August 1, 2021, http://www.as.utexas.edu/~wheel/africa/namoratunga.htm.

35. Eric Betz, "Nabta Playa: The World's First Astronomical Site Was Built in Africa and Is Older than Stonehenge," *Discover,* June 20, 2020, https://www.discovermagazine.com/the-sciences/nabta-playa-the-worlds-first-astronomical-site-was-built-in-africa-and-is.

36. Michael Palin, *Sahara* television series, quoted in "100 Things That You Did Not Know about Africa," *Black History Studies,* 2009, http://www.blackhistorystudies.com/resources/resources/100-things-about-africa/.

37. Audrey Bennett, "The African Roots of Swiss Design," *The Conversation,* March 22, 2021, https://theconversation.com/the-african-roots-of-swiss-design-154892. See also Bennett, "Follow the Golden Ratio from Africa to the Bauhaus for a Cross-Cultural Aesthetic for Images," *Journal of African Art History and Visual Culture* 6, no. 1 (January 10, 2014), https://www.tandfonline.com/doi/abs/10.1080/19301944.2012.10781414.

38. "African Architecture," *Culturally Situated Design Tools* (CSDT), accessed April 7, 2021, https://csdt.org/culture/africanfractals/architecture.html.

39. "100 Things That You Did Not Know."

40. "100 Things That You Did Not Know."

41. John Lienhard, "No. 385: African Steel Making," *The Engines of Our Ingenuity,* University of Houston, 1990, https://www.uh.edu/engines/epi385.htm.

42. "100 Things That You Did Not Know."

43. Ross Jones, "Borgu History," accessed on August 9, 2011. Unfortunately this website appears to have been decommissioned.

44. Londa Schiebinger, *The Secret Cures of Slaves: People, Plants, and Medicine in the Eighteenth-Century Atlantic World* (Stanford, CA: Stanford University Press, 2017), 50.

45. Schiebinger, *The Secret Cures of Slaves,* 50–51.

46. Schiebinger, *The Secret Cures of Slaves,* 51.

47. "100 Things That You Did Not Know."

48. Carvalho and Harris, "Africa Before," 17.

49. "100 Things That You Did Not Know."

50. "The Oldest University in the World," Erudera, https://erudera.com/resources/oldest-universities/. For other sources focused on this embattled subject, see "Ancient Higher-Learning Institutions," Wikipedia, https://en.wikipedia.org/wiki/Ancient_higher-learning_institutions, accessed December 7, 2022.

51. David Adamo, *Africa and the Africans in the Old Testament* (Benin City, Nigeria: Justice Jeco Press and Publishers, 2005).

52. Adamo, *Africa and the Africans in the Old Testament*, 179.

53. Adamo, *Africa and the Africans in the Old Testament*, 180.

54. Adamo, *Africa and the Africans in the Old Testament*, 180.

55. Adamo, *Africa and the Africans in the Old Testament*, 180. For an impressive list of other military, economic, and administrative roles and positions that Africans played or occupied in Israeli society, see 181–183.

56. Antonio C. S. Rosa, "Civilized, Barbarians, Savages," *Transcend Media Service*, March 23, 2020, https://www.transcend.org/tms/2020/03/civilized-barbarians-savages/.

CONCLUSION: TWO VIEWS OF HUMANITY

1. James Allen Rogers, "Darwinism, Scientism, and Nihilism," *Russian Review* 19, no. 1 (January 1960): 16, http://www.jstor.org/stable/126189.

2. Rogers, "Darwinism, Scientism, and Nihilism," 22.

3. Ashley Montagu, *Darwin, Competition and Cooperation* (New York: Henry Schuman, 1952), 48–69. Cited in George E. Simpson, "Darwin and 'Social Darwinism,'" *Antioch Review* 19, no. 1, *The Origin of Species, 100 Years Later* (Spring 1959): 42, http://www.jstor.org/stable/4610123.

4. Simpson, "Darwin and 'Social Darwinism,'" 42.

5. Gary Kohls, "The 102nd Anniversary of the Christmas Truce of 1914: Questioning Christian Participation in Aggressive War," *Transcend Media Service*, December 26, 2016, https://www.transcend.org/tms/2016/12/the-102nd-anniversary-of-the-christmas-truce-of-1914-questioning-christian-participation-in-aggressive-war/.

6. Kohls, "The 102nd Anniversary."

7. Kohls, "The 102nd Anniversary."

FIGURE CREDITS

Figure 1.1. Charles Darwin caricatured as an "orang-outang" by the satirical magazine *The Hornet* in 1871. Public Domain.

Figure 2.1. Representatives of the European powers at the Berlin Conference in 1884–85 as depicted in German newspaper *Illustrierte Zeitung*. Public Domain.

Figure 3.1. Lord and Lady Lugard in 1908. Public Domain.

Figure 3.2. Sir Charles Eliot, Commissioner of British East Africa. Public Domain.

Figure 3.3. Social Darwinist Benjamin Kidd promoted an evolutionary account of human development in his book *The Principles of Western Civilisation* (1902). Public Domain.

Figure 3.4. Sir William MacGregor, Governor of Lagos Protectorate, Nigeria, from 1899–1904. Public Domain.

Figure 4.1. Racist chart from 1912 depicting the "progressive development" of human races. In John Clark Ridpath, *With the World's People*, vol. 1 (Cincinnati, OH: Jones Brothers Publishing, 1912), 233. Public Domain.

Figure 5.1. The Islamic Emir of Katsena from Northern Nigeria on his visit to England in 1921. In J. A. Hammerton, *Peoples of All Nations*, vol. 1 (London: The Educational Book Co., 1923), 519. Public Domain.

Figure 6.1. Missionary Walter Miller with two Hausa students from Northern Nigeria in 1925. Published in *Reflections of a Pioneer* by

W.R.S. Miller (Church Missionary Society, 1936). Public Domain or Fair Use.

Figure 6.2. Bishop Samuel Ajayi Crowther, the first African Anglican bishop in Nigeria, opposed the monopolistic practices of the United African Company. Public Domain.

Figure 7.1. Cover of *Native Races and Their Rulers: Sketches and Studies of Official Life and Administrative Problems in Nigeria* (1918) by Charles Lindsay Temple. Public Domain.

Figure 8.1. Hausa woman trader. In J. A. Hammerton, *Peoples of All Nations*, vol. 1 (London: The Educational Book Co., 1923), 558. Public Domain.

Figure 9.1. Comparison of human and gorilla skeletons, late nineteenth century. ©Archivist/Adobe Stock.

Figure 9.2. Anatomy of the human eye. ©Natalia/Adobe Stock.

Figure 9.3. Anatomy of the human ear. ©Stockshoppe/Adobe Stock.

Figure 10.1. Hausa musicians in Nigeria. In J. A. Hammerton, *Peoples of All Nations*, vol. 1 (London: The Educational Book Co., 1923), 559. Public Domain.

Figure 11.1. Multiracial group holding each other's hands. ©TheVisualsYouNeed/Adobe Stock.

Figure 12.1. Stele of the ancient African kingdom of Axum, fourth century AD. I, Ondřej Žváček, CC BY-SA 3.0 via Wikimedia Commons.

INDEX

CPSIA information can be obtained
at www.ICGtesting.com
Printed in the USA
LVHW041152290123
738032LV00002B/7

9 781637 120231